P9-BJU-316

JX
1952
.H85
1972

Huxley, Aldous Leo-
nard

An encyclopaedia
of pacifism

The
Garland Library
of
War and Peace

The
Garland Library
of
War and Peace

Under the General Editorship of
Blanche Wiesen Cook, *John Jay College, C.U.N.Y.*
Sandi E. Cooper, *Richmond College, C.U.N.Y.*
Charles Chatfield, *Wittenberg University*

An Encyclopaedia
of Pacifism

edited by
Aldous Huxley

with a new introduction
for the Garland Edition by
Milton Birnbaum

Garland Publishing, Inc., New York & London
1972

Library of Congress Cataloging in Publication Data

Huxley, Aldous Leonard, 1894-1963, ed.
  An encyclopedia of pacifism.

  (The Garland library of war and peace)
  Reprint of the 1937 ed.
  Includes bibliographies.
  1. Peace. 2. Pacifism. I. Title. II. Series.
JX1952.H85 1972   327'.172   70-147443
ISBN 0-8240-0233-4

Introduction

Aldous Huxley's encyclopedic interests led him to comment on a seemingly endless number of subjects — from acupuncture to Zen Buddhism. Coming from one of Europe's most distinguished families (his genealogy includes Matthew Arnold, Thomas Henry Huxley, Mrs. Humphry Ward, and Dr. Thomas Arnold of Rugby fame; his brothers and half-brothers number among them a brilliant biologist and a Nobel Prize winner in physiology), and educated and trained in both the sciences and the arts, Huxley observed life's diversities and paradoxes and analyzed extensively what he perceived. Although admittedly an introvert preferring the perusal of a volume of the Encyclopaedia Britannica *(his favorite reading) to posing as a* salvator mundi, *he nevertheless felt compelled by his conscience to try to bring some sanity into a world increasingly eroded by the disasters of overpopulation, exploitation of natural resources, and the recurrence of sectional and global wars. His* Encyclopaedia of Pacifism *can best be evaluated by a consideration of Huxley's lifetime preoccupation with war and peace.*

When World War I broke out, Huxley tried to enlist several times but was rejected each time because of his poor eyesight.[1] In a letter to his brother

Julian Huxley in March of 1916, he wrote: "The longer this war goes on, the more one loathes and detests it. At the beginning I shd. [sic] have liked very much to fight: but now, if I could (having seen all the results), I think I'd be a conscientious objector, or nearly so." [2] *Whatever incipient endorsement he had given to the war by trying to enlist in the armed forces disappeared quickly as the war dragged on and its destructiveness and futility became apparent. By the end of the war, Huxley was clearly a pacifist, a role he maintained until his death.*

In his first novel, Crome Yellow *(1922), he wrote with the kind of Swiftian irony so typical of his fiction in the 1920s and 1930s that "Those who had lost relations in the war might reasonably be expected to subscribe a sum equal to that which they would have had to pay in funeral expenses if the relative had died at home."* [3] *In* Point Counter Point *(1928), he created a witheringly satiric portrait of a would-be totalitarian leader in Everard Webley (whose prototype is the British fascist, Sir Oswald Mosley); although to Huxley the nationalism of any governmental leader, democratic or otherwise, was a contributing cause of war, he quite rightly felt that totalitarian mentalities had a more sinister effect.* Brave New World *(1932) is more concerned with satirizing the dehumanizing effects of a technological Utopia, yet in the character of Mustapha Mond, one of the world's twelve controllers, Huxley gave a picture of the archetypal wielder of power — and war has a tendency to produce this kind of ruthless monstrosity.*

Although Huxley held power-mad leaders of government responsible for the initiation and the waging of war, he did not by any means exculpate the masses of people (those that President Nixon would call "the great, silent majority"). In After Many a Summer Dies the Swan *(1939), he observed that so long as people worship false idols like money and material success they will be victimized by war. Similarly in* Time Must Have a Stop, *he wrote:*

> *Without Susan and Kenneth and Aunt Alice and all their kind, society would fall to pieces. With them, it was perpetually attempting suicide. They were the pillars, but they were also the dynamite; simultaneously the beams and the dryrot. It was thanks to their goodness that the system worked as smoothly as it did; and thanks to their limitations that the system was fundamentally insane — so insane that Susan's three charming babies would almost certainly grow up to become cannon fodder, plane fodder, tank fodder, fodder for any one of the thousand bigger and better military gadgets with which bright young engineers like Kenneth would by that time have enriched the world.[4]*

And what a monstrous futility wars are! As Eustace Barnack, a character in the same novel, contemplates past wars, he recalls the terrifying discrepancy between intention and result:

He remembered his collection of Historical Jokes. A

million casualties and the Gettysburg Address, and then those abject, frightened negroes one sees in the little towns of Georgia and Louisiana. The crusade for liberty, equality, fraternity, and then the rise of Napoleon; the crusade against Napoleon; and then the rise of German nationalism; the crusade against German nationalism, and now those unemployed men, standing, like half-animated corpses, at the corners of mean streets in the rain.[5]

His pacifist sentiments were not confined to fiction. As war became imminent in the 1930s, Huxley, like many other well-intentioned intellectuals, overcame his natural tendency to avoid public involvement and declared himself actively for pacifism. In 1935 he addressed a gathering held under the auspices of the London and Middlesex Quarterly Peace Committee and the London Center of Friends Service Council. In this talk, entitled "Pacifism and Philosophy," he pointed to the dangers of the verbal abstractions employed by military propagandists (abstractions such as "the state," "the nation," "war of attrition," etc.); these abstractions tend to hide the basic destructiveness of war in clouds of verbal ambiguity. He also demonstrated his loss of faith in "humanism" as a viable philosophy for peace because "humanists" have, over the centuries, abetted the waging of wars. As he was to do for the remainder of his life, he endorsed a belief in a "spiritual reality at once transcendent and immanent":

Humanism doesn't work and so is pragmatically untrue.

8

INTRODUCTION

> *There are, of course, other grounds for regarding humanism as an unsatisfactory doctrine and for believing in the existence of a spiritual reality at once transcendent and immanent, in which all human beings are united .... Equally unpropitious is any kind of superhumanism that lends itself to exclusiveness and division. There is left the belief in a spiritual reality to which all men have access and in which they are united. Such a belief is the best metaphysical environment for pacifism.[6]*

His most dedicated declaration of the wisdom of pacifism and the destructive banalities of war is found, however, in his Encyclopaedia of Pacifism, *written for the Peace Pledge Union. In 1934 Canon H. R. L. Sheppard invited all men who opposed war to send him a postcard indicating their complete renunciation of war; the response was overwhelming and, eventually, the Peace Pledge Union grew into an organization of almost 150,000 men and women who worked with Continental and American pacifists for "constructive peace" by organizing meetings, publishing a weekly* Peace News, *and doing everything in their means to stave off the outbreak of conflict by establishing the conditions in which peace could flourish. Besides Huxley, the sponsors included many people whose names are forgotten today, and also people like the novelists Storm Jameson and Rose Macaulay, the poet Siegfried Sassoon, and Bertrand Russell, who became more famous for his political activism than for his contributions to mathematics and philosophy. Huxley wrote "the first official pamphlet of the Movement,"* What Are You Going to Do About It? The Case for Constructive Peace, *and later edited* An Encyclopaedia of Pacifism *(subsequently incorporated in revised form into Chapter IX of his* Ends and Means*).*

This little "encyclopaedia" has fifty-four sections arranged alphabetically from "Armaments, Private Manufacture of" to "Women in Modern War, Position of," with the longest sections being devoted to "Defence," "Non-Violence," "The Peace Pledge Union," and "War Resisters' International." There are some curious entries, such as "Shelley," in which Huxley describes how Shelley was inspired to write his Mask of Anarchy. *Some sections are of historical importance only – for example, "Disarmament Conference," "League of Nations," "Mandates" (as administered by the League of Nations), and "Sanctions" (again, applied by the League of Nations). Apparently written in great haste and more with an eye for journalistic simplicity than with a view towards profound permanence, it contains such platitudes as the following: "In the meantime we must do everything we can to secure a decent standard of life for every human being" (p. 27), and sloganeering – as found in the section on "Consumers' Co-operative Movement," whose guidelines are "Production for Use, Not for Profit," "Government by the People for the People," "Each for All and All for Each" (p. 29).*

Occasionally, Huxley's reasoning seems naïve at

best and distortedly superficial at worst. For example, in his section "International Politics in the Light of Christ's Teaching," he attributes the fall of Jerusalem to the Jews' refusal to bow down to Roman dictates: "To the policy [of Jesus] the Jews preferred armed revolt; the Romans reacted against violence with violence, and, since they were the stronger, Jerusalem was sacked, even as Jesus had predicted" (pp. 62-3). By the same line of reasoning, World War II would never have taken place if only England and France and Russia had bowed down to Hitler's desires. Similarly, in arguing that militant statements by Jesus were probably spurious, he assumes that "the principle that the more unconventional the sayings of Jesus are the less likely are they to be later, or edited, is a sound one" (p. 19). It would be just as logical to assume the opposite since Huxley offers no proof for his own assumption. He refers to the thoughts of Confucius and Lao Tsu but omits mention of pacifist statements of Isaiah and Zechariah.

Again, he displays at times an extraordinary innocence as when in giving us "The Moral Equivalent for War" (a title for one of his sections which is clearly borrowed from an earlier work by William James, who is never mentioned in the book), he writes that the principles of obedience, courage, and self-sacrifice, sometimes induced by war, can be adequately obtained in peace by having young people engage in such activities as "fire-brigade service,

INTRODUCTION

life-boat service, lighthouse service, sea-fishery, mine safety work, down to traffic direction, and sewer inspection" (p. 72, emphasis added). The latter inclusion would tempt the reader to believe that Huxley had forgotten that he was writing a serious work rather than engaging in satiric fiction. More fundamentally, he fails to realize that protest meetings, publications (open and clandestine), individual and group conscientious objection to war have never really had much success in preventing the waging of warfare; his belief that reason and good will can seriously affect the likes of Hitler and his Nazis seems to offer a picture of benign ineffectuality rather than a meaningful program for achieving a viable peace. He had once criticized Sigmund Freud for being blind to the existence of Menos, "the state of mind-body that leads to success" and overemphasizing Ate, "the state of mind-body that leads to disaster." [7] In expecting most people to listen to reason, Huxley seems blinded by Menos and not sufficiently aware of Ate.

And yet these criticisms do not destroy the essential value of either the book or the man. The postmortem dissection is always more sagacious than a diagnosis of an existing crisis and a prognosis of what to do about it. There are many sections in the book whose value has outlasted the 1930s. His analysis of the causes of wars, his belief that wars cannot be curtailed by one method alone but rather by a total attack on all the causes of war (psychological, propagandistic, political, etc.), his

12

great courage in asserting that it takes more courage in being pacifist than belligerently patriotic, his lucidity in style and the clarity of organization of his materials — all these make his Encyclopaedia of Pacifism *a worthwhile addition to any library concerned with war and peace.*

Furthermore, since Huxley continued to be preoccupied with the question of war and peace for the rest of his life, he had sufficient perception to admit the mistakes in his Encyclopaedia *and to offer alternative paths for the elimination of war. In a letter to Mrs. Flora Strousse written in 1941, he writes that "it is clear that to make peace now with the Germans on their terms will lead to catastrophic results."* [8] *But this belief did not in any way make him give up his belief in pacifism; although both he and his first wife wanted to become American citizens, they refused to swear to defend the Constitution — not on the religious basis of conscientious objection to war but rather on the scruples of philosophical morality. Thus, "Huxley finally let the applications lapse. He and his wife were technically never 'refused' American citizenship."* [9] *Similarly, the vitality and relevance of Huxley's position on war can be seen in an observation he made to John Atkins in 1955: "I don't think that the pacifist position will ever be generally accepted on religious or ethical grounds — but it may be forced on the world by the logic of technological advance. Meanwhile the best way to further peace is (for a*

13

writer) to call attention to the psychological and demographic factors making for war." [10]

That Huxley himself realized that some of the assumptions he had made in his Encyclopaedia *were more optimistic than realistic can be seen in a letter he wrote to Anthony Brooke in 1961. Here he no longer claims as he did in 1937 that a study of biology does not reveal the preponderance of aggressive instinct in man; instead, he notes, "The great mistake that vitiated all earlier studies of animal behaviour was the assumption that most conflicts between sub-human creatures were fights about food or about sex. This assumption is simply not true. The ethologists of the last 30 years have accumulated a mass of material from which it is quite clear that most animal conflicts are about* status *and about* property, *private or collective. Animals behave instinctively much more like power politicians and ambitious status-seekers, than like heroes of romance doing battle for the love of a fair lady."* [11] *Because man is bestial and irrational, the cures for war will no longer rest on the blithe assumption that most people can be reasoned with; angelic panaceas simply will not work with instinctively aggressive and irrational forces.*

His last published novel, Island *(1962), attempted to reconcile the contributions of Eastern Buddhism with the Pavlovian conditioning of Western science. Like B. F. Skinner (despite Huxley's reference to the utterances of J. B. Watson and Skinner as*

14

INTRODUCTION

"preposterous" and "such rot" [12]), he opted for benign conditioning of man by a wisely Utopian government in preference to the illusion of individual freedom; yet Huxley's basic honesty would not let him substitute a euphoric hope for what he recognized as unpleasant truth. It is not the yoga-inspired idealists who are going to take over the island of Pala (his Utopia in the novel) but rather the sinister fascistic forces of Colonel Dipa.

It would seem then that Huxley's vision of attaining a peaceful world remained just that — a vision, but who would deny him the vision and choose instead to be confronted exclusively by the spectacle of inescapable brutality? It is the vision of men like Huxley which enables us to endure reality and to continue to strive for amelioration, elusive though it may be. Every prophetic vision deepens our perspective and thus enhances our ability to improve. It is indeed as Huxley wrote in 1941: "The world would be even more horrible than it actually is, if it were not for the existence of a small theocentric minority working along quite other lines than the anthropocentric majority." [13]

To this "theocentric minority," Aldous Huxley definitely belongs — with distinction.

Milton Birnbaum
Department of English
American International College
Springfield, Massachusetts

15

INTRODUCTION

NOTES

[1] *Ronald W. Clark,* The Huxleys *(New York and Toronto: McGraw-Hill Book Co., 1968), p. 168.*

[2] *Grover Smith ed.,* The Letters of Aldous Huxley *(New York: Harper & Row, 1969), p. 97.*

[3] Crome Yellow *(New York: George H. Doran Co., 1922), p. 181.*

[4] Time Must Have a Stop *(New York and London: Harper & Bros., 1944), p. 279.*

[5] Ibid., *p. 193.*

[6] *Arthur and Lila Weinberg, eds., "Pacifism and Philosophy,"* Instead of Violence, Writings by the great advocates of peace and nonviolence throughout history *(New York: Grossman Publishers, 1963), p. 179.*

[7] Literature and Science *(New York: Harper & Row), pp. 88-89.*

[8] The Letters of Aldous Huxley, *p. 470.*

[9] Ibid., *p. 691 n.*

[10] Ibid., *p. 781. For other comparable expressions on war and peace, see his* Science, Liberty and Peace *(1946).*

[11] The Letters of Aldous Huxley, *p. 924.*

[12] Ibid., *p. 847.*

[13] Ibid., *p. 470.*

AN
ENCYCLOPÆDIA
OF PACIFISM

Edited by

Aldous Huxley

128 PAGES • 55 ARTICLES • PRICE 6d.
CHATTO & WINDUS

AN
ENCYCLOPÆDIA
OF PACIFISM

Edited by
ALDOUS HUXLEY

—

1937
Chatto & Windus
LONDON

PUBLISHED
under the auspices of
THE PEACE PLEDGE UNION
96, Regent Street
London, W.1
by
Chatto & Windus
LONDON
and
The Macmillan Company
of Canada, Limited
TORONTO

An
Encyclopædia of Pacifism

Armaments, Private Manufacture of

The desire of arms manufacturers to make profits is a standing menace to world peace. It is in their interest to work for policies which are likely to produce dangerous international situations and to work against disarmament and the establishment of world peace, which would spoil their trade.

This trade is a very profitable one. Between 1915 and 1918 the American munition firm of Dupont de Nemour paid dividends amounting to 458 per cent of the part value of the original stock. According to British history of the Ministry of Munitions, the profits of J. P. Morgan & Co. amounted, from 1914 to 1918, to more than $2,000 million. Recently British rearmament has brought substantial profits to manufacturers and especially financiers. In the *Daily Telegraph* of March 11, 1935, we read that Vickers Ltd. is giving a free three-fourths share for every six-eighth share held. The ordinary dividend for 1935 was raised from 6 per cent to 8 per cent. Writing in the *Peace Year Book*, Mr. Francis Williams estimates that the total profit to armament share interests during

1935 was more than £32 millions. More than £5 millions of this went into the pockets of the promoters who floated new aircraft companies.

The cynically anti-social attitude of the arms manufacturer is well expressed in the following remark, which is cited from an article in *The Aeroplane* for March 15, 1933. "The manufacturers of both aeroplanes and engines may hope for increased turnover and profits a year or so hence, when the Disarmament Conference has faded out and the programme of expansion is allowed to proceed."

In a Memorandum addressed to the Admiralty in 1919, Admiral of the Fleet Lord Wester Wemyss summed up the case against the arms manufacturer as follows: "Every firm engaged in the production of armaments and munitions of any kind naturally wants the largest output. Not only has it a direct interest in the inflation of the Navy and Army Estimates and in war scares, but it is equally to its interests to push its foreign business. For the more armaments are increased abroad, the more they must be increased at home. This interrelation between foreign and home trade in armaments is one of the most subtle and dangerous features of the present system of private production. The evil is intensified by the existence of international armament rings, the members of which notoriously play into each other's hands. So long as this subterranean conspiracy against peace is allowed to continue, the possibility of any serious concerted reduction of armaments will be remote." In the United States an inquiry into private arms manufacture was held in 1934 and 1935, and in England a Royal Commission sat in 1935. Private manufacture still continues.

2

For the arms manufacturer, profit comes before patriotism. He will sell his products to anyone who is prepared to buy, even though the buyer be an actual or potential enemy. In his evidence before the Arms Commission (1935) Mr. W. Arnold Forster mentioned the fact that a gun captured by the Bedfords in Palestine had the words "Made by Sir W. G. Armstrong Whitworth & Co." inscribed on it.

Agreement between arms manufacturers may even survive the outbreak of hostilities. During the World War, the Briey basin was not bombarded, because French and German armament makers had a gentlemen's agreement that neither side should be embarrassed in its production of munitions. The war was consequently prolonged; but the profits of the manufacturers were increased.

That armament firms may take active steps to sabotage attempts at disarmament was demonstrated in the notorious Shearer case. In 1929 Mr. Shearer sued the three largest American shipbuilding companies for a quarter of a million dollars for services rendered at the Geneva Naval Conference of 1927. (They had already paid him fifty thousand dollars.) His duties at the Naval Conference were as follows: to work up fear of the British Navy by means of anti-British propaganda; to entertain naval officers and newspaper correspondents; to get big-navy publicity into reputable American journals in the guise of news; to discredit American peace organizations. Meanwhile, at home, he was to organize a lobby at Washington for the purpose of influencing federal legislation in favour of a big navy and merchant marine; he was to have articles inserted in magazines, and lectures and addresses delivered before patriotic organizations, American Legion branches,

3

Chambers of Commerce, etc. In brief, Mr. Shearer's business was, by all means in his power, to make it appear that the interests of the Bethlehem Shipbuilding Corporation, the Newport News Shipbuilding and Drydock Company, and the American Brown Boveri Corporation, were identical with the interests of the American people. (Cf. *Patriotism Ltd.* published by the Union of Democratic Control.)

The two points to notice here are these:

(1) Industrialists and financiers brought up in the capitalist ethic will behave (probably with a perfectly clear conscience) in ways that are morally outrageous and socially mischievous.

(2) Ordinary people, who stand to make no profit out of war, can be swept off their feet by bellicose propaganda, however discreditable its origin. Exploiters and Exploitees are equally the victims of their upbringing in a society which esteems above everything success, possessions, triumph at the expense of others. Not only the economic system, but also what may be called the psychological system of our societies requires changing. The two are related, and yet in some measure independent of one another. A desirable change in the economic system would not automatically produce a change in the psychological system sufficiently great to make war impossible. That is why it is essential that there should be associations of men and women specifically pledged to put pacifist principles into action in all the circumstances of life: in personal relations, in economic relations, in politics, in education.

(See *Arms Trade, Nationalization of; Economic Reform and Pacifism; Education and Peace.*)

4

Armaments Race

The two points to be noticed in regard to the Armaments Race are the following:

(1) All statesmen insist that the armaments of their own nation are being prepared solely for reasons of defence.

(2) All statesmen insist that the existence of armaments in a foreign country constitutes a reason for the immediate creation of new armaments at home.

"Germany is making her preparations not in order to *attack* anyone, but to insure that no one shall be able to attack or bully our country again" (Dr. Rudolf Kircher, Editor of the *Frankfurter Zeitung*, in a letter to the *Spectator*, November 11, 1936).

"We should never use our forces for aggression. They threaten no-one, and no-one is afraid that they do. We do not desire forces greater than are necessary for our own defence and to enable us to fulfil our responsibilities" (Mr. Neville Chamberlain in a speech at Kelso, September 21, 1935).

Such quotations could be multiplied indefinitely. Every nation is defending itself against the defensive measures of all the other nations. (See *Example.*)

Arms Trade, Nationalization of

The private manufacture of armaments is morally disgraceful, and at the same time, as has been shown in the article on the subject, politically dangerous. Reformers have, therefore, proposed that the manufacture of armaments should be entirely nationalized. (In recent years the State has manufactured about five-twelfths of the armaments used by Great Britain—private firms about seven-twelfths.) This would certainly liberate governments from the influence of socially irresponsible profit-makers. But it must not be imagined that nationalization is a complete solution of the problem. Private manufacture of armaments is morally outrageous and politically dangerous; but so, in its own way, is the manufacture of armaments by the nation.

(1) Instruments of murder are always instruments of murder, whether privately or publicly manufactured.

(2) State manufacture would give a certain legal sanction to the production of these instruments. The mass of unthinking public opinion would feel that an officially sanctioned armament industry must somehow be respectable. The total abolition of the evil thing would consequently become more difficult.

(3) Nationalization of the armament industry would lead to an undesirable strengthening of the already too powerful authority.

(4) The State is more powerful than any private employer. The personnel of a nationalized arms industry could be dragooned and bribed so as to become a kind of technical army at the disposal of the executive.

(5) The armament industries of highly industrialized States would be in a position to supply or withhold war material from less-developed States. In this way it would be possible for States with efficient arms monopolies to exercise political pressure upon their neighbours. (See *Economic Reform and Pacifism*.)

Nationalization of armament manufacture is merely the substitution of one evil for another. What is needed

6

is complete abolition.   If machinists, railway workers and dockers were to refuse to co-operate in the manufacture or transport of armaments, and if this movement were supported by a refusal to co-operate in the production of militaristic propaganda on the part of the writers, printers and teachers, the iniquitous preparations for mass murder would soon be effectively brought to a stop.   (See B. de Ligt, *Mobilisation contre toute guerre*.)

Biology and War

War is often described as a Law of Nature.   This is not true.   Among the lower animals war is unknown. True, there are carnivores which prey upon other animals; but their activities are no more war-like than are the activities of fishermen or butchers.   Moreover, the existence of carnivores should not blind us to the fact that there is at least as much co-operation in nature as strife.

Individuals of the same species often fight together; but these fights are seldom pushed to a finish; the conquered is rarely killed or even permanently hurt.   Such duels waged in the heat of passion, under the stress of hunger or sexual impulse, are quite unlike war, which is mass murder, scientifically prepared in cold blood.

In nature, it is only among the social insects, such as the ants and termites, that we meet with anything resembling war.   And even here the resemblance is only superficial. Insect wars are conducted by members of one species against members of another species.   Man is the only creature to organize mass murder of his own species.

It is often argued that war is inevitable, since man is

7

descended from pugnacious ancestors, akin to the gorilla. This is probably not the case. Most zoologists are now of the opinion that man's ancestor was not a gorilla-like ape, but a gentle, sensitive creature, something like a tarsier. In any case, the gifts which brought man his extraordinary biological success were not ruthlessness and brute strength (plenty of animals are much stronger and fiercer than he is), but co-operation, intelligence, wondering curiosity and sensitiveness. In the words of Charles Darwin, "The small strength and speed of man and his want of natural weapons are more than counterbalanced, firstly, by his intellectual faculties (chiefly or exclusively gained for the benefit of the community), and secondly, by those social qualities which led him to give and receive aid from his fellowmen."

Another biological argument often invoked in defence of war is the following: War is civilization's equivalent of natural selection; it acts as nature's pruning-hook, ensuring the survival of the fittest. This is obviously untrue. War tends to kill off the young and healthy and to spare the unhealthy and those who are too old to beget children. In the second place, there is no reason to suppose that warlike peoples are superior to unwarlike peoples. Even if the violent were to survive (and war is just as likely to kill them off as to ensure the persistence of their stock), this would not necessarily mean the survival of the most satisfactory type of human being. The most violent are not the best human beings; nor, conversely, are the most valuable necessarily the strongest. In so far as war is an agent of selection it selects dysgenically, ensuring the survival, not of the more desirable, but of the less desirable human strains. In the past war's capacity to

8

do harm was limited by the fact that the instruments of destruction at men's disposal were crude and inadequate. To-day, thanks to technological progress, they are enormously efficient. War, therefore, has now become as dangerous to human societies, and even to the whole human species, as cancer is to the human body. War is "natural" to exactly the same extent as cancer is "natural."

British Empire

An area comprising about one-quarter of the land surface of the world, and about one-quarter of its population, which is either controlled by, or associated with, Great Britain, and which occupies this position as a result of various historical causes. Chief among these causes are (a) that we were victorious in the great wars of the sixteenth, seventeenth and eighteenth centuries; (b) that we preceded all the other nations in the development of the modern industrial system, which creates a demand for markets and fields of investment outside the mother-country, and so led to the imperialist aggressions of the nineteenth century.

The claims of British colonists to self-governing institutions, which caused the loss of the American colonies in 1782, raised a problem which was solved, partially at least, by granting self-government to Canada, Australia, New Zealand, and the white population of the Union of South Africa.

There are, therefore, speaking broadly, two distinct parts of the Empire: (a) a "White Empire," which might fairly be called a "Commonwealth of Nations," comprising

9

a population of about 65 millions, and (*b*) a "Dark Empire," which is ruled from above with about 385 millions. In effect, there is a Commonwealth ruling an Empire; though in India, Burma, Ceylon and the West Indies some steps have been taken towards self-government for the "Dark" populations. (See *Mandates; Imperialism and Colonies; Defence.*)

British Influence,
Effect of Pacifism on

It is often stated, as an argument against pacifism, that a disarmed Britain would lose all influence in world affairs and that, since this influence is an influence for good, the world would suffer. Britain should be strong for the benefit of humanity in general.

In regard to this contention we may make the following remarks:

(1) The identical argument was used by Hitler to justify German rearmament. A weak Germany, he proclaimed, was a source of general insecurity; a strong Germany would be a blessing for the whole world. We regard Hitler's argument as a tissue of sophistries. Why should our own exactly similar argument deserve to be regarded differently?

(2) All countries regard themselves as virtuous; all take it for granted that any war in which they take part will be a war of defence, not of aggression; all believe that it is only the imperialism of other nations that is bad. British aims, motives and methods are not regarded by others with the same admiration as we give to them

10

ourselves. We may think that the influence which our enormous navy allowed us to exercise throughout the world was wholly good; others are not of this opinion. The truth of the matter would seem to be that any imperialism, including our own, is bad.

(3) British influence upon the world was based upon sea power. Because Britain was invulnerable and because the British Navy controlled the seas, we were able, during the eighteenth and nineteenth centuries, to add colony to colony, to seize strategic ports and establish naval bases and coaling stations throughout the world. In narrow seas the navy is now an ineffective instrument. Sea power has therefore lost most of its significance. If we imagine that we can continue to have the kind of influence that was ours during the nineteenth century, we are cherishing an illusion. The foundations of that power—domination of the sea—have slipped away from under us. The game of imperialism is one which, whether we like it or no, we are no longer in a position to play. To make believe that we are what we were during Queen Victoria's reign is merely silly. The facts of the contemporary world are such that we cannot hope to go on having the kind of influence we once possessed.

(4) If we really wish to exercise a beneficent influence upon the world (and, incidentally, at the same time to save our own country from irremediable ruin) we should do all in our power to induce the government to get rid of its armaments and either to liberate outright its subject people or else, where this did not seem practicable, to hand over the administration of them to a genuinely international authority. Such a policy would do more for peace than any other that a British government could

pursue. Our present policy, which consists in combining vulnerability at home with menaces abroad, is a policy that fairly invites war—a war in which, owing to the rise of air power, we shall suffer more than any other nation. Menacing rearmament is our surest way of losing whatever influence we ever possessed; disarmament, even unilateral disarmament, is our surest way of regaining influence—a genuinely beneficent influence for peace. (See *Defence*.)

Causes of War

The main causes of war are of three kinds: (1) the pursuit of wealth, (2) the pursuit of glory, (3) the advocacy of a creed. Usually all three are combined in varying proportions, as, for example in the Book of Joshua. The economic motive has various forms:

(a) Occupation of fruitful territory—e.g. Whites and Indians in United States.

(b) Plunder—e.g. Romans in Asia Minor; Cortez and Pisarro.

(c) Trade—e.g. English and Dutch in seventeenth century.

(d) Markets and fields for investment—most modern imperialist wars.

(e) Raw materials—e.g. Japan in China, France and Germany as regards Lorraine.

The motion of glory is usually dynastic or governmental—for example, the ancient Assyrians and Persians, and eighteenth-century wars so far as the Continent of Europe is concerned. But it can be made popular by propaganda, and always has been made so since the French Revolution.

Creed wars may be religious or political; usually they are both. They almost always also have economic motives. The early Mohammedans, for example, had economic motives (*a*) and (*b*); the Protestants wished to secure church lands and revenues; and so on. The English Civil War combined religious and political motives in equal measure. The Albigensian crusade was, on the part of the instigators, more economic than political. The French revolutionary wars, the American Civil War, and the various civil wars since 1815, involved important politico-economic issues, and were all, in a greater or less degree, creed wars.

The main causes predisposing to modern war are: first, the competition between States for markets and raw materials; secondly, the competition between classes as regards the distribution of the national wealth. These two causes are intertwined, because different governments stand for different economic systems. (See *Economic Reform and Pacifism; Education and Peace.*)

Chemical Warfare

During the Crimean War Lord Dundonald proposed that sulphur fumes should be used against Sebastopol. The War Office rejected the proposal on the grounds that "an operation of this nature would contravene the laws of civilized warfare."

Gases much more poisonous than sulphur fumes were used in the last war, first by the Germans, then by all the combatants. In 1925 the Powers met at Geneva and signed a Protocol completely prohibiting the use of gas in warfare. It is clear, however, that no nation considers itself bound by its pledges in this matter. Chemical research is carried on by the military authorities in every country. Everywhere it is taken for granted that, in the next war, open towns will be subjected to intensive chemical bombardment from the air. The Geneva Gas Protocol of 1925 is treated in advance as merely a scrap of paper.

The principal chemicals used in the last war were as follows:

Chlorine. The gas first used by the Germans. Attacks the air cells of the lungs.

Chloropicrine. Attacks lungs and eyes. It is a liquid and, when scattered, continues to give off poisonous vapours for many hours.

Phosgene. Similar to chloropicrine, but more poisonous. From the military point of view it is not very satisfactory as it is a gas, not a liquid; consequently does not poison the ground, but is blown away by the wind.

Mustard Gas. This is a liquid and can contaminate ground for days and even weeks. Two or three hours after exposure to mustard gas the patient begins to cough and vomit; his eyes are inflamed; his throat is parched. Next the skin begins to itch and large blisters form all over the body. At the end of the first day "the patient lies virtually blinded, with tears oozing between bulging œdematous eyelids." After the second day acute bronchitis develops. Second-day infections then set in, causing broncho-pneumonia. Death occurs at any date from the second day to the fourth week. "With ill-protected

14

troops the death-rate may be very high." (*Note.*—The civilian population is not protected at all.)

Lewisite. Similar to mustard gas, but more poisonous, owing to its arsenic content. It has been calculated that fifty bombers each carrying five thousand pounds of Lewisite could, under perfect conditions, poison an area fifty miles long and thirty-five miles wide.

Thermite. A mixture of powdered aluminium and iron oxide. When ignited, rises to a temperature of 5000° centigrade—nearly as hot as the surface of the sun. A small thermite bomb, no bigger than a cricket ball, is enough to start a fire. A single plane could carry many hundreds of such bombs.

All the foregoing substances were known in 1918. Much research has been devoted to chemical warfare since that date and it is certain that considerable improvements have been made both in the substances themselves and in the methods of using them.

How is it proposed to defend civil populations against chemical attacks?

In 1932 Mr. Baldwin said: "The only defence is in offence, which means that you have to kill women and children more quickly than the enemy if you want to save yourselves." In 1936, Colonel Lindbergh affirmed that there was now no such thing as a defensive war. It is significant that the main increase in the Air Force is an increase in bombers—that is to say in instruments of aggression, not of defence.

Meanwhile, there is talk of gas masks, gas drill, and the like. Gas masks cannot be worn by young children, by the aged, or by those with any weakness of the lungs. Moreover, even if they could be supplied to all those physically capable of wearing them, they would be perfectly useless against Mustard Gas or Lewisite, which do not affect the lungs alone, but the entire body. Why should an enemy obligingly use chemicals against which some protection exists, when he can drop other substances against which there is no protection?

A bombardment with a mixture of thermite, high explosives and vesicants would kill large numbers outright, would lead to the cutting off of food and water supplies, would smash the system of sanitation and would result in general panic. There would be a frantic rush out of the towns. Those who were not crushed to death in this first rush would die of starvation and disease later on. The chief use of the army would be, not to fight an enemy, but to try to keep order among the panic-stricken population at home.

China, Pacifism in

Confucianism holds up the ideal of the just, reasonable, humane and cultivated man, living in an ordered and harmonious society. Europeans have always unduly admired the military hero and the martyr. Not so the Chinese. "The traditional conception of Confucianism," writes Max Weber, "tends to prefer a wise prudence to mere physical courage and to declare that an untimely sacrifice of life is unfitting for a wise man." The European preference for military heroism and martyrdom is a most unfortunate one; for it has tended to make men believe that death was more important than life and that a long course of folly and crime could be cancelled out

16

by a single act of physical courage.   In this way it has
provided justifications for every kind of atrocity, from
religious persecution to aggressive imperialism.   Plato
was of the same opinion as Confucius.   "Many a mer-
cenary soldier will take his stand and be ready to die at
his post; and yet they are generally and almost without
exception insolent, unjust, violent men and the most
senseless of human beings."   To die courageously is less
important (though of course a man should be ready, if
necessary, to sacrifice his life in a noble cause) than to
live humanely, harmoniously, intelligently.   Such is the
teaching of Confucianism.

Confucius was a rationalist.   Lao Tsu, or whoever was
the author of the *Tao Te Ching*, was a mystic.   The Tao,
or way, is an eternal, cosmic principle, which is at the same
time the inmost root of the individual's being.   Philosophically, the doctrines expressed in the *Tao Te Ching*
are akin to those current in Indian thought.   Its ethical
teachings—the command to return good for evil, to culti-
vate humility, to refrain from assertiveness and self-
importance—are similar in many respects to those of Jesus.

Since the time of Confucius and Lao Tsu, Chinese
ideals have been essentially pacific.   European poets have
glorified war; European theologians have sanctified religious persecution and nationalistic aggression.   This has
not been the case in China.   Chinese religion, whether
Confucian, Taoist or Buddhist, has always been anti-
militarist.   So have the majority of the great Chinese
poets.   The soldier was regarded as an inferior being,
not to be put on the same level with the scholar or the
administrator.

The Chinese have shown themselves capable of carrying

17

out very effective non-violent resistance to aggression. During the World War, for example, Japanese aggression was resisted by non-co-operation in the form of a boycott of Japanese goods. In 1925 a number of Chinese students were shot by British troops. The reply was a boycott which caused the English to lose nearly three-quarters of their trade with China.

In recent years the great tradition of Chinese pacifism has shown signs of weakening. China is being Westernized. This means, in practice, that its inhabitants are being supplied with modern weapons, conscripted (the law was promulgated in 1936) and drilled. (See *Christ, The Teaching of; Christian Church's Attitude to War, The; India, Pacifism in.*)

Books: the most complete history of Pacifist ideas and practice is *La Paix Créatrice,* by B. de Ligt, published by Marcel Rivière, rue Jacob, Paris.

Christ, The Teaching of

For the teaching of Christ in regard to war and the overcoming of evil the chief authorities are the several elements which are contained in the Synoptic Gospels, the relevant passages in St. Paul's Epistles and such evidence as can be found elsewhere in the New Testament. His teaching has been too frequently sought only in isolated sayings divorced from their setting and interpreted as legislative enactments. But for Christians who believe that His intention was never legislation, that His character is a consistent whole, and that His authority depends upon the quality of His person and the spirit of His actions rather

18

than upon isolated and edited utterance, it is more important to consider the significance of His crucifixion than to debate particular points, such as the alleged use of a whip in the Temple-market (John ii, 15), or the cryptic and despairing "It is enough!" (Luke xxii. 38), or the parable of the strong man armed—who is obviously the devil! (Luke xi, 21).

In any case it is not easy as the whole record of the Church's attempts to justify war proves (the *Summa Theologiæ* falls back upon a quotation from John the Baptist) to quote any authority from Christ. If we appeal to isolated sayings, such words as "Do not offer violence in opposing evil" (Matt. v, 39) which St. Paul explains by adding, "But overcome evil with good" (Rom. xii. 21), or "They that take the sword shall perish by the sword" (Matt. xxvi. 52), are at once more explicit and more representative: and the principle that the more unconventional the sayings are the less likely are they to be later, or edited, is a sound one. For those who cling to the supposed sanction of one or other of the familiar "pro-war" sayings Dr. G. H. C. MacGregor's recent volume provides a full examination of them.

In considering the general meaning of Christ the following points are surely indisputable: (1) He regarded God as always and everywhere the Father whose dealings with His creatures are motivated only by love: to assert that God uses alternative methods—love and justice—and that love is not always applicable is to deny either that God is what Jesus taught or that He is in any real sense God. (2) In consequence men are persons, not pawns or slaves, and their freedom to reject must never be overborne by force whether of violence or of bribery or of the supernatural.

19

At His temptation (Matt. iv. 1–11, Luke iv. 1–13) Jesus repudiated these three ways of coercing men. The method of His whole ministry is consistent with this repudiation; He rejected the nationalist policy of the Zealots, the cheapening and materializing of His own demands, the use of psychic or miraculous powers to enforce assent. (3) In presenting His call to His people He refused to admit either by resistance or by flight that the last word lay with armed force: indeed, by accepting the Cross He challenged this common assumption and disproved it. Non-resistance, seeming at first to fail, actually and signally triumphed. His crucifixion transformed His disciples and changed the course of history. The Cross, the symbol of non-resistance, has been, however, inappropriately, the Church's sacred emblem ever since.

The new way of life thus initiated was accepted and proclaimed by the earliest disciples. Love, joy, peace, fortitude were acknowledged as the fruit of Christ's spirit: martyrdom was the Christian answer to militarism: warfare was with the powers of evil—of the spirit not of the flesh. The only book in the New Testament that shows evidence of another way, the Revelation, is a product rather of Jewish apocalyptic than of Christian patience, and was in fact regarded as non-canonical by the best minds of the early Church. For them military service was a thing impossible: violence was condemned: and war was an outrage against God. (See *China, Pacifism in; Christian Church's Attitude to War, The; India, Pacifism in*.)

Christian Church's Attitude to War

Contrary to the widely-held and oft-repeated view that Jesus Himself gave no verdict on the rightness or wrongness of war, it is clear on several grounds that He was convinced of its wrongness, and that He taught, acted, and suffered accordingly. Several conditions, however, impeded the clear grasp of this verdict on the part of His early followers; for example, the remoteness of the whole question (as a practical issue) from the lives of most of them, their consequent absorption in many more immediate spiritual and moral questions, the war-stories in Scripture, the difficulty of seeing how the Emperor (regarded by all as God-ordained) could get on without an army, and the tendency of simple-minded Christians to take the line of least resistance in face of a complex problem. Hence, during the first three centuries, we see two processes going on side by side: (1) the expansion of the Church leading first to the conversion of soldiers who remained soldiers, and then to the enforced or even voluntary enlistment of Christians in the army: and (2) the Christian ethic of love making it increasingly clear to the thoughtful Christians that the profession of Christianity was incompatible with a military life. There probably existed a few Christian soldiers from the very first, but we do not hear of them in any numbers until A.D. 170. Most early Christian authors, on the other hand, speak of gentleness, bloodshed, etc., in such a way as to suggest that, if consistent, they must have held that no Christian could fight: yet we find no explicit mention of this precise issue till A.D. 177–80, when Celsus' attack on Christianity seems to presuppose a general refusal on the part of Christians to serve in the legions. This refusal was expressly approved and defended by Tertullian (even in his pre-Montanist days), Hippolytus, and Origen in the third century, and Lactantius early in the fourth century. Of these the most significant is Origen, who writes as if a refusal to fight were the normal Christian position, bases this refusal not on any dread of contamination from idolatry, but on Jesus' ethical teaching, and defends it (with a theory of the special function of Christians in the world) against the current charge of incivism. Round about A.D. 300 we get cases of men punished for refusing, when required, to serve as soldiers: the best known is that of Maximilian, martyred in Northern Africa in A.D. 295.

When Constantine became supreme in A.D. 313, the Church was so grateful to him for delivering her from prolonged and crushing persecution and for graciously and generously patronizing her, that it would have been exceedingly difficult—even if her mind had been clearly and unanimously made up—for her to adhere to a strictly pacifist attitude. As Christian feeling was far from being unanimous, such an adherence was out of the question. There is no need to doubt the sincerity of Constantine's conversion: but his alliance with the Church necessarily committed her to a willingness to allow lay-Christians to fight under him and his successors. This turnover in conviction did not indeed come all at once. During the fourth century, individual Christians refused service, individual writers expressed approval of such refusal, and—more significant still—certain codes of Church-procedure in the East still maintained the old pacifist rigour. But, broadly speaking, the case had gone by default. Henceforth, for many centuries—though from time to time the

22

Church exerted herself in the cause of peace—the only surviving trace of the Origenist position was the rigid refusal to allow *the clergy* to shed blood in war: but ways were found now and then for evading even this restriction. The refusal of a layman to serve as a soldier became a mark of heresy: it was one of the characteristics of the Cathari or Albigenses, who were so mercilessly persecuted in the thirteenth century.

When the Reformation came—early in the sixteenth century—the return to Biblical religion re-opened the problem. Erasmus gave a strong lead by his eloquent denunciations of war. Luther at first was strongly inclined to a strict obedience to the Sermon on the Mount: but he entirely gave this up (except as purely abstract theory) after 1525, and taught that Christians must accommodate themselves to the needs of an imperfect world so far as to fight when required. Calvin, by a different theoretical route, arrived at a similar result even less reluctantly. The pacifist practice was, however, maintained by the Anabaptist groups up and down Europe, and defended both by them and by Faustus Socinus. Its positive service to human progress was totally overlooked. It was felt to be socially so dangerous that it greatly embittered the persecution to which Anabaptists and Socinians were subjected by both Catholics and Protestants.

Since the sixteenth century, pacifist practice has been maintained for the most part only by comparatively small non-Catholic sects—such as the Doukhobors in Russia, the Mennonites in the Low Countries, and the Quakers in England. Individuals in other Protestant bodies have from time to time revealed the uneasiness of the conscience of Christendom by advocating pacifism as the truly Christian way: but it was not until the Great War (more particularly the introduction of conscription in England) that Christian men on any large scale were roused to face the issue afresh. The conscientious-objection-movement, and all the discussion that has gone on concerning it since 1914, has introduced a fresh chapter in the history of Christian ethics, and necessitated a deeper consideration of the issues involved than has ever been given to them since the days of Origen.

Civil War

Societies cannot hold together without traditional loyalties and habits of confidence, kindness and forbearance. More even than international war, civil war destroys these essential conditions of a tolerable social life. England has had no foreign invasion since 1066 and no considerable revolution since 1688. That is why democratic institutions have been able to flourish here. They cannot flourish in countries where civil wars are frequent.

Once civil war has actually begun, it is hard for the pacifist to act with much effect. He must therefore do all he can, while peaceful conditions prevail, to prevent civil war from ever breaking out. He must refuse to join political parties pledged to intolerance and the persecution of their enemies; and he must do his best to dissuade others from joining such parties.

If the pacifist finds himself confronted with the *fait accompli* of civil war, what should be his policy? In his

24

pamphlet on Spain, Mr. Runham Brown has written on this problem as follows. "I am not opposed to the use of a certain measure of physical force; but that force must be a restraining force and not a destructive one. . . . If I found that the reactionaries were in such numbers or possessed of such weapons as to make restraint impossible and that mass destruction was the only means of subduing them, I should definitely reject that method, even if I had to allow them to take control; but if they did take control, it would not be with my help. I should refuse them all co-operation, refuse to become their tool and should use my best efforts to bring everything to a standstill." Summing up, we may say that the pacifist's policy in regard to civil war should be as follows: pacification of mutually intolerant groups in time of peace; restraint of the war-makers at the first outbreak of civil strife; then, if that proved impossible without mass murder, non-co-operation. (See *Revolution.*)

Class War

The pacifist does not ignore the existence of the so-called Class War in modern capitalistic society. Nor is he indifferent to it. Without necessarily accepting the Marxian analysis of our social order, it is evident that just as there are "Haves" and "Have-Nots" among the nations, so there are among the social strata within the nations. The wealthier and more powerful classes tend to live by the exploitation of their fellows. Such a state of affairs is contrary to pacifist principles. It involves

25

moreover much unnecessary suffering and even death through conditions of starvation or semi-starvation, inadequate precautions against accidents (because these would involve a reduction of profits), sweated employment, etc. Modern industry takes a huge toll of life and health, most of which could be avoided. Employers exercise economic power over employees (which is essentially non-moral). Friction and hatred result.

The pacifist's sympathy is naturally with the exploited and the down-trodden. The spirit of the class war and particularly any recourse to violence in the furthering of it are, however, anathema to him. He must seek a solution of the social conflict along other lines. An important step forward is to show to all concerned that the idea of the class war is based on conditions which no longer exist. In a world of economic scarcity, the wealth of one group means the poverty of another. But we live in an age of potentially unlimited plenty. There is, therefore, no economic reason for the class struggle. There is however a psychological factor. Some men desire power over others. This lust for power is the principal source of evil and it is essential to combat it by every means, psychological as well as political. The educational system must be so designed that it shall turn children into free and responsible human beings, not into militarists. (See *Education and Peace.*) Executive power must be decentralized, so that there shall be genuine democracy and widespread self-government. (See *Political Implications of Pacifism.*) The economic power in the hands of individuals must be limited and the principle of co-operation extended. (See *Economic Implications of Pacifism, Consumers' Co-operative Movement, The.*) The

26

power-religions of nation, race and class must be combated. (See *Nationalistic Religion.*) In the meantime we must do everything we can to secure a decent standard of life for every human being.

In the social struggle, as in the international field, the problem needs deep study of possible ways of transforming our present chaotic system into an orderly one based on the pacifist principle of co-operation for the common good. As in the international field, the technique of non-violence will prove the most effective weapon. (See *Civil War; Economic Implications of Pacifism.*)

Communism and Fascism

The way in which violence begets violence is very clearly illustrated by the history of the rise of Communism and of Fascism. The Communist revolution in Russia was the fruit of violence. Tsarist tyranny had prepared the ground, sowing hatred and resentment among the oppressed masses. In 1917 the fabric of Russian society had been reduced to chaos by the impact of war. Military violence gave the revolutionaries their opportunity; violently, they seized it. More military violence, in the shape of the White Russian and allied attacks upon the Bolshevists, confirmed the new régime in its essentially anti-pacifist principles. Marxian theory had from the first insisted upon the necessity of violence; but even if they had not desired to do so, circumstances would have compelled the Bolsheviks to put the Marxian theory of violence into practice. Communism became a militant, even a militaristic creed.

27

Communist violence in Italy, itself produced in large measure by the disruptive violence of war, evoked violent reaction. Fascism was born and, after a period of civil strife, came to power

In the case of Germany, the allies were given ample opportunity to behave with justice and generosity; but, during the fifteen years which preceded the accession of Hitler, Germany was treated with consistent injustice. Such concessions as were made were always made reluctantly and so late that they never did anything to allay the bitterness of German public opinion. In Nazism, Frenchmen and Englishmen are reaping the fruits of their governments' stupid inhumanity and injustice. Hitler's violence is the answer to the arrogance of France and England and, to a less extent, to the militant propaganda of Russian Communism—itself, as we have seen, a product of earlier violence.

Anti-Communists call upon us to suppress Communism by violence; anti-Fascists exhort us to answer the threats of Nazism with counter-threats. Both parties would have us reply to violence with violence. In other words both would have us do precisely those things which, as the history of the last twenty years makes so abundantly clear, are certain to produce the greatest possible amount of tyranny, war and civil strife. Pacifists are people who profit by the lessons of history; militarists, whether of the right or the left, are people who are determined not to learn by experience. (See *Revolution; Civil War.*)

Consumers' Co-operative Movement

The Consumers' Co-operative Movement must not be confused with the "Army and Navy" or any other stores. Nor must it be looked on as just a prosaic method of thrift, nor dismissed because of its imperfections.

It is, as a matter of fact, an economic and ethical revolution, and a colossal structure, existing in over thirty countries, for carrying on trade and industry by organized consumers. It is built up by working-class capital, and is therefore free from capitalist control and speculation.

The watch-words of the Movement are "Production for Use, not for Profit," and "Government by the People for the People." Its motto is "Each for All and All for Each."

What is familiarly known as the "divi" is the method by which capitalist profit-making is abolished, because the surplus on trading does not go to the owners of capital, but is in the main (after paying a fixed interest on capital) returned to the purchasers according to the amount of their purchases.

The British and Irish Movement has $7\frac{1}{2}$ million members. Membership of local "Co-ops" is open to everyone who takes up a £1 share (payable by instalments). Shares are withdrawable and no one can hold more than 200. Members elect the Management and other Committees, and, through the Quarterly Meetings, control the general policy. Voting is on the principle of "one person, one vote," whatever the number of shares held.

These societies form a network over nearly the whole of the country. In 1935 their trade was nearly £221 millions. They have proved a valuable check on the raising of prices by local rings, for example, in bread, coal and milk. In the milk trade, they have been the pioneers in many places of the latest hygienic methods. Most societies give grants for education and recreation, amounting in 1935 to over £251,000. Since these figures were published, striking progress has been made; for example, in London (which was a co-operative desert in 1900) a trade of £28 millions is done by about $1\frac{1}{4}$ million members.

The distributive societies have formed themselves into *Federations* for national purposes, with thoroughly democratic constitutions. On the trading and manufacturing side, the most important are the English, Scottish and Irish *Co-operative Wholesale Societies*. Their trade amounted in 1935 to nearly £$117\frac{1}{2}$ millions. The English C.W.S. also carries on Banking and Insurance at its headquarters in Manchester, the Mecca of Co-operators from all over the world. Its soap production makes a breach in the Soap Monopoly. Altogether the C.W.S. is the largest business dealing in domestic supplies in Britain. It has carried on friendly trade and other relations with the Russian Co-operators for the last fifteen years.

The Co-operative Union deals with legal matters, parliamentary legislation, propaganda, agriculture, etc. It holds the Annual Co-operative Congress of delegates from affiliated societies. Its educational work comprises a College, with training for teachers, research and statistical work.

An additional feature of the educational and propaganda doings of the movement is the un-official "Guilds," the largest of these being the Women's Co-operative

Guild, with nearly 80,000 members. It is recognized by the official bodies, but is independent in its action. It has specialized in rank and file co-operative education and policy, and on the reforms needed in married working women's lives, for example, its successful campaign for a co-operative women's minimum wage and for Maternity Benefit. It strongly supports complete pacifism.

The British Movement which employs about 300,000 workers has a good record as regards hours and wages. It originated the weekly half-holiday in shops, pays trade union (or higher) wages; and the C.W.S. and many of the large societies require their employees to be trade unionists; there is a system of arbitration in disputes. It is a splendid stand-by for the workers in lock-outs and strikes.

Owing to capitalist attacks, co-operators have formed a political party and entered Parliament, where they work with the Labour Party.

The Co-operative Press publishes a variety of periodicals, including the *Co-operative News*, and it now owns *Reynolds' News*, the old radical Sunday paper.

A world-wide Federation, the International Co-operative Alliance, has been formed by the movements of thirty countries, laying the foundation of an Economic League of Peoples. It was the only organization which maintained contact with all its members during the War. (See *Economic Implications of Pacifism*.)

Cost of War

The cost of the Great War has been reckoned at about four hundred thousand million dollars, or eighty thousand million pounds. According to figures quoted by Dr. Nicholas Murray Butler in his 1934 report to the Carnegie Foundation this sum would have sufficed to provide every family in America, Canada, Australia, Great Britain and Ireland, France, Belgium, Germany and Russia with a five-hundred pound house, two hundred pounds worth of furniture, and a hundred pounds worth of land. Every town of twenty thousand inhabitants and over in all the above-mentioned countries, could have been presented with a library to the value of a million pounds and a university to the value of two millions. After which it would have been possible to buy the whole of France and Belgium, that is all the land, houses, factories, railways, churches, roads, harbours, etc., in these countries. In 1914 the total value of France was, according to official statistics, sixty-two thousand million dollars; the total value of Belgium, twelve thousand million dollars. This means that, with the money required to impose the Treaty of Versailles upon Germany, one could have bought, lock, stock and barrel, five countries as large as France and five others as large as Belgium. To impose this same Treaty of Versailles thirteen millions of human beings were killed outright, while war conditions were responsible for the death of many millions more.

Defence

Most military experts are agreed that it is impossible to defend large cities, such as London or Birmingham, against attack from the air. A cynically frank article in the *Army, Navy and Air Force Gazette* informs us how the fighting forces regard our anti-aircraft defences. "However completely we may guard our country in the air, it is more than likely that enemy bombers will get through. If they are permitted to carry out destruction unimpeded, the great danger is that the will of the people to continue the struggle, which is the mainspring of victory, will give way. If, on the other hand, the searchlights are playing and the guns are banging, they will not feel that they are the victims of Government incompetence and neglect as well as of unprovoked aggression, and will be willing to continue the struggle." The guns must bang, not because the banging will prevent women and children from being massacred, but because the noise will encourage people to go on with the war, that is, consent to the massacre of yet more women and children.

Anti-aircraft guns and interceptor planes cannot prevent all the bombers from reaching their destination. (Air-Marshal Sir Robert Brooke Popham goes so far as to say that "in the next war enemy aeroplanes will only meet one another by accident or by mutual design.") Some of the raiders will doubtless be brought down; but enough will get through to spread death, destruction and panic. The chief result of anti-aircraft fire and interceptor attack will be to make the raiders drop their bombs hurriedly and therefore inaccurately. An unopposed raid might, if the raiders so desired, be directed against

33

particular military objectives, such as government offices, barracks, aerodromes, factories, railway stations and the like. An attack opposed by guns and interceptors would not be stopped, it would merely be made indiscriminate. In their anxiety to get out of the danger zone, raiders will content themselves with dumping their fire and poison at any point on the enormous targets spread out beneath them. By compelling raiders to fly higher than they would otherwise do, balloon barrages will produce the same results as anti-aircraft guns and interceptors. So will black-outs. From a great height you cannot trace the topography of a darkened city in detail; but you can see the city as a whole. All the anti-aircraft defences hitherto devised guarantee only one thing; that the aerial bombardment shall have the maximum of imprecision— in other words, that the civil population, and not any specifically military objective, shall be the principal target.

It may be remarked that defences against land attack tend to produce the same results. Thus, there is reason to believe that the Maginot line of fortification which guards France's eastern frontier and which is now to be extended to the Channel, is practically impregnable. If the Germans were to attack France, would they waste their resources in storming defences which cannot be taken? Obviously not. The very strength of France's purely military defences makes it certain that any attack against her will be directed against the civil population from the air. The existence of the Maginot line is the guarantee that in any future war Paris will be bombed.

In a recent series of articles the military correspondent of *The Times* pointed out that, so far as land warfare is concerned, the power of defence has increased more rapidly than the power of attack. It is unlikely that a land offensive could succeed against troops armed with the weapons which modern technology has placed at their disposal. This being so, it is obvious that strategists will not waste their resources in attempting the imposssible. They will strike where the enemy's armour is weakest—that is to say, at the civil population in large cities.

Because it is an island, because it is not self-supporting, because it is densely populated, England is more vulnerable than any other European country. Paris and Berlin are far from the frontiers of France and Germany; London, a far larger city, is situated within a few miles of the frontier of England. Most of our food comes from abroad, and the ships carrying it have to pass through narrow seas which no navy can defend from air attacks. One port, that of London, supplies a quarter of the whole population. Nothing would be easier than to paralyse the port of London. If this happened, those eleven millions who are fed from London would have to subsist on accumulated supplies. But the accumulated supplies of food in this country are very small and most of them are stored at the ports, where they could be destroyed easily.

As things are at present we combine the maximum of vulnerability (due to our geography and the distribution of our population) with the maximum of potential aggressiveness (due to our armament policy). We are more open to attack than any other nation and we now ourselves are trying to make ourselves more formidable than others as a potential attacker. Our new air-fleets contain far more bombers than interceptors, that is, far more instruments of attack than instruments of defence. Our whole defence policy is based on the threat of aggressive retaliation.

But, in the nature of things, we cannot inflict as much damage on an enemy as the enemy can inflict upon us. Foreign populations are not so dense as our own; foreign capitals are smaller and farther from the frontier than is London. Numerical parity and even numerical superiority in the air would do nothing to diminish our intrinsic vulnerability. In any war of aggression and counter-aggression, we should inevitably come off worse than any of our potential enemies or allies. And we should come off worse, even though our air-fleet might be larger than theirs. Our present policy, which consists in combining vulnerability with aggressive rearmament, is merely suicidal.

A Genuine Defence Policy. At least a year's supply of food must be kept in store and, to avoid the danger of destruction, the stores should be in small granaries scattered widely over the countryside. Essential services should be duplicated, dispersed and protected. Fire-fighting services should be enlarged and a corps of technicians organized for repairing damages done. Finally, the heavy industries should be decentralized and the cities rebuilt, so as to consist of a series of tall blocks of buildings, each with its bomb-proof roof and each standing in its area of open space. This rebuilding would provide a fair measure of security from air attack and would, at the same time, vastly increase the amenity of our at present monstrously ugly, unhygienic and inefficient cities. The expense would, of course, be very great, but not much greater than the expense of aggressive armaments and

36

incomparably less than the expense of the war which those armaments invite.

Meanwhile, our huge fleet of bombers should be completely scrapped. By reducing simultaneously our vulnerability and our power of aggression, we should make it quite clear that we were concerned solely with our own legitimate defence. In this way, we should make a real contribution towards the safety of our people and the peace of the world. A well-defended, unaggressive Britain would not provoke attack nor offer a temptingly easy target.

Along with these purely technical measures would have to go a complete reorientation of policy. It is clear, for example, that a hopelessly vulnerable Great Britain cannot expect to preserve a large colonial empire for its own exclusive benefit. During the nineteenth century, when our command of the sea was undisputed, we followed the policy of the open door. During the twentieth, when sea power has lost most of its importance and when, from being the least vulnerable country in Europe, we have become the most vulnerable, we have chosen to place barriers in the way of free trade. Such a policy is an invitation to other nations to attack us. Its reversal is desirable not only on moral grounds, but also as a simple measure of national self-preservation.

The conclusions we have reached may be summed up as follows:

(1) Existing passive defence methods serve only to make attack indiscriminately destructive.

(2) Our policy of defence by means of threatened attack can only serve to alarm foreign nations and ultimately to invite aggression; for, however great our air

forces, we cannot, owing to the facts of geography, inflict as much damage as can be inflicted on us.

(3) Technical measures for passive defence can be taken. Pacifists may legitimately support a policy of genuine defence without aggression.

Disarmament Conference

The associated powers who were victorious in the Great War promised in Article 8 of the Covenant, incorporated in the Treaty of Versailles (1919), that the Council of the League would "formulate plans" for "the reduction of national armaments to the lowest point consistent with national safety and the enforcement by common action of international obligations." But it was not till 1932 that the question of an all-round reduction of armaments was referred by the League of Nations to an international conference for consideration. The Disarmament Conference, over which The Right Hon. Arthur Henderson was selected to preside, first sat in February 1932 and continued its deliberations for over two years, the last full session being held in June 1934. A tentative draft agreement drawn up previously by the British Government in which many blanks were left to be filled in came under discussion, attempts were made to differentiate between offensive and defensive armaments and various suggestions were made for the limitation of armaments and for the abolition of certain war weapons. The Soviet suggestion of complete disarmament had been ruled out of order at a preparatory conference held before the Disarmament Conference itself had been convened.

38

It soon became clear that with the aid of the experts who attended the conference anything like a unanimous decision on any point was impossible. The discussions showed clearly that an attempt was being made not to prevent war but to decide how the next war should be waged.

The powers were beginning at the wrong end. Armaments depend on policy and until the causes of war have been examined and complaints, claims and grievances have been fully stated, it is useless to lay down arms regulations which would certainly be broken by any nation which imagined itself in danger.

Economic Implications of Pacifism

Constructive pacifism is more than a mere objection to war; it is a complete philosophy of life, and as such has important political, sociological and economic implications. The capitalist system is essentially militaristic. Competition between small profit-making enterprises may be compared to inter-tribal warfare. The rise of the huge company and the amalgamation of companies into trusts and cartels are phenomena analogous to the emergence of national communities. There is conflict between these large economic groups, just as there is conflict between nations. There are also treaties of alliance, made for the purpose of exploiting the consuming public. At this point the analogy with nationalism ceases to hold good. Singly or in groups, nations fight with one another; there is no common enemy against whom they can all combine. For capitalist concerns, a common enemy exists in the shape of the consumer. They can make peace and come together in order to despoil that common enemy.

Pacifists are equally opposed to the inter-tribal conflicts of small competitive concerns, to the large-scale conflicts of great trusts (conflicts which, when the trusts are organized on a national crisis with the support of the national government, are the preliminaries of military warfare between nations), and to the exploitation of that common prey of all profit-making enterprises, the consumer. Capitalism, at any rate in its present socially irresponsible form, is incompatible with pacifist principles. The philosophy of pacifism insists that to employ good means is of greater practical importance than to pursue good ends. This is so, because good means can only result in good ends, whereas good ends cannot be achieved by bad means. Pacifists reject the revolutionary's theory that violence and tyranny are justified when used for a good cause. On this point they part company with communists, fascists and all others who believe that the world can be bludgeoned into the likeness of Utopia. Their political philosophy is democratic.

Some few attempts have already been made to modify the militaristic character of capitalism, to limit opportunities for private profit-making and to protect the consuming public. The London Transport Board and the Port of London Authority are essays in the limitation of capitalism. The Post Office, municipal services for transport, light, water, roads and the like are examples of full-blown socialism already at work. The Co-operative Movement has shown that, without violence and even without the backing of state or municipality, private individuals can create, in the midst of capitalist surroundings, a flourishing island of non-competitive, non-exploiting, non-profit-making economic activity. Co-operation is applied pacifism. The more widely the application can be made the better. In the British Isles co-operation has tended to confine itself too narrowly to the preparation and distribution of foodstuffs. The experiments in the various Scandinavian countries have, however, made it clear that the principle can be extended much more widely. To increase the membership and enlarge the activities of the Co-operative Movement is work of an essentially pacifistic nature. (See *Consumers' Co-operative Movement; Economic Reform and Pacifism; Revolution.*)

Economic Reform and Pacifism

The causes of war, it is often argued, are predominantly economic; these causes cannot be removed except by a change in the existing economic system; therefore pacifist movements, like the P.P.U., are useless.

Those who use such arguments belong to two main classes: currency reformers and socialists.

(1) Currency reformers, such as Major Douglas and his followers, point to the numerous defects in our present monetary system and affirm that, by remedying those defects, prosperity could be made universal and war eliminated. This is over-optimistic. Defects in the monetary system may intensify economic conflicts in general. But by no means all economic conflicts are conflicts between nations. Many of the bitterest economic conflicts are between rival groups within the

same nation; but because these rival groups feel a sentiment of national solidarity, their conflicts do not result in war. It is only when monetary systems are organized in the interests of particular groups of nations that they became a potential cause of war. So long as nationalism exists, scientifically managed currencies may actually make for war rather than peace. "Once the controllers of national monetary systems begin to apply their power self-consciously for the betterment of their people, we have monetary conflicts arising on strictly national lines, such as we see to-day in competitive exchange depreciation and exchange control" (quoted from *Economic Cause of War*, by Kenneth Boulding). The greater the conscious, scientific control exercised by national monetary authorities, the greater the international friction, at any rate until such time as all nations agree to adopt the same methods of control.

(2) The present economic system is unjust and inefficient, and it is urgently desirable, as the socialists insist, that it should be reformed. But it must not be thought that such reforms would automatically lead to universal peace. "In so far as the socialization of a single nation creates truly national monopolies in the exports of that nation, so the power of the government increases, and the national character of economic conflicts becomes intensified. Thus the socialization of a single nation, even though the rulers of that nation be most peaceably minded, is likely to intensify the fears of other nations in proportion as the control of the socialist government over its country's economic life is increased. . . . Unless they are supported by a strong conscious peace sentiment, they (the socialist régimes of individual

42

nations) may be turned to purposes of war just as effectively—and indeed probably more effectively—than capitalist societies." It will thus be seen that pacifist movements have an important part to play. That changes in the present system must be made is evident; and it is also clear that, in the long run, these changes will make for the establishment of peace. But meanwhile, so long as nationalistic sentiment persists, reforms in the economic and monetary system may temporarily increase international ill feeling. The function of pacifist movements is to prevent, if possible, the desirable changes in the economic and monetary systems from resulting in discord. To renounce war personally and to stand by that renunciation is the best propaganda that individuals can make in favour of peaceful internationalism and against a nationalism that may be bellicose even under a socialist régime.

Economic Warfare

The causes of war are of various kinds, political, economic, psychological, etc., but it is clear that at the present time the economic factor is a very important one. The struggle for markets and for raw materials is openly declared by governments to be the reason for their war preparations, and has been an important factor in the several wars which have been waged during recent years. The desire of certain nations to obtain colonies is partly a matter of prestige, but partly also a matter of economic necessity. It is useless to say that such and such a country does not need colonies because it can freely buy all the raw materials it needs in the world's markets. Actually

43

it is often unable to do so. Its currency is unacceptable beyond its own frontier and the world supply of gold is ludicrously inadequate for the amount of modern international trade. Goods can only be paid for by goods. Imports must be balanced by exports. But when such a nation seeks to export its manufactured goods, it is met everywhere by tariff barriers which make its task an impossible one.

There are 7,000 miles of new tariff-walled frontiers in Europe since the War. Everywhere tariffs have steadily increased, often as measures of economic retaliation. The British Empire, which in pre-war days was a free-trade Empire, where all nations could buy and sell on equal terms, is now a tariff-bound territory, in which nations outside the Empire are at a considerable disadvantage.

Quotas and restrictions add their effect to tariffs in strangling international trade, and countries without colonies feel the effect of this in a steady forcing down of their standard of life. In such circumstances even the manufacture of armaments may appear to have an economic justification in increasing the home market and lessening unemployment, quite apart from their use as an international bargaining weapon, or their use in a war for colonial territory.

The tariff war, which has been raging in the world for the past fifteen years and shows little sign of becoming less acute, is a potent cause of international friction which is leading to war. Although the world's economic experts have repeatedly declared that there can be no return to prosperity without a lowering of tariff barriers, no government is prepared to take the first step. In

44

tariffs, as in armaments, a policy of example is needed. Britain might well take the lead by giving to all nations equal trading rights in those territories over which she has control (i.e. India, the Crown Colonies and the home country). It is significant that discriminatory tariffs are forbidden in the mandated territories. The alternative to economic disarmament (if necessary unilateral), is the continuation and intensification of tariff war until it produces armed conflict. (See *Example; Haves and Have-Nots.*)

Education and Peace

In totalitarian states all education is avowedly an education for war. The military training of children in these countries begins almost before they are out of the kindergarten. The period of compulsory military service at eighteen or twenty is merely the culmination of an educational process which has been going on for years.

Military discipline and training in the use of arms is accompanied by a training in nationalistic fervour. This is carried out mainly by means of the teaching of history. The art of distorting history in favour of one's own country or race has been carried to extraordinary lengths under the dictatorships. Young Germans are taught that art, science, philosophy and ethics are purely Aryan and Nordic products; young Italians are taught to worship the Roman Empire; young Turks learn that the world owes its civilization to the Seljuks. And so on.

To a less extravagant degree, the same is true even of the liberal democracies. History, as taught in English and French schools, for example, is history with a strong national bias. Even when the facts are not distorted, they are selected—and the selection is in favour of militarism. Thus, in a *History of Great Britain and Ireland* for use in lower forms, sixty-six pages out of one hundred and sixty dealt with wars, while only one page was given to the Industrial Revolution, and three-quarters to social conditions after 1815. Trades Unions, Co-operative Societies and the Labour Party were not mentioned at all; nor, except for Chartism, was there any reference to any working-class movement of the nineteenth and twentieth centuries.

Nationalism is the most powerful of contemporary religions, and in all countries children are systematically instructed in the tenets of the local nationalist creed. Like the Jesuits and, more recently, the psycho-analysts, the rulers of modern states realize the importance of catching the human animal while it is young and plastic.

In the education of children, the manner of teaching is at least as important as the matter taught. Dr. Montessori, the pioneer of modern pedagogical methods, has written on this subject as follows: "The child who has never learned to act alone, to direct his own actions, to govern his own will, grows into an adult who is easily led and must always lean upon others. The school child, being continually discouraged and scolded, ends by acquiring that mixture of distrust of his own powers and of fear, which is called shyness and which later, in the grown man, takes the form of discouragement and submissiveness, of incapacity to put up the slightest moral resistance. The obedience which is expected of the child both in the home and in the school—an obedience

46

admitting neither of reason nor of justice—prepares the man to be docile to blind forces. The punishment, so common in schools, which consists in subjecting the culprit to public reprimand and is almost tantamount to the torture of the pillory, fills the soul with a crazy, unreasoning fear of public opinion, even of an opinion manifestly unjust and false. In the midst of these adaptations and many others which set up a permanent inferiority complex, is born the spirit of devotion—not to say of idolatry—to the "condottieri," the leaders. . . ." Dr. Montessori might have added that the inferiority complex often finds expression in compensatory brutality and cruelty. The traditional educational methods are calculated to form a hierarchical society in which people are abjectly obedient to their superiors and inhuman to their inferiors. Each slave "takes it out of" the slave below.

Bertrand Russell has an interesting paragraph in his book, *Which Way to Peace?* on the relation between education and militarism. "Schools," he writes, "have very greatly improved during the present century, at any rate in the countries which have remained democratic. In the countries which have military dictatorships, including Russia, there has been a great retrogression during the last ten years, involving a revival of strict discipline, implicit obedience, a ridiculously subservient behaviour towards teachers and passive rather than active methods of acquiring knowledge. All this is rightly held by the governments concerned to be a method of producing a militaristic mentality, at once obedient and domineering, cowardly and brutal. . . . From the practice of the despots, we can see that they agree with the advocates of 'modern' education as regards the connection between discipline in schools and a love of war in later life."

It is a significant fact that Montessori methods are discouraged and even prohibited in the principal dictatorial countries. The Montessori Society of Germany was dissolved by the political police in 1935; and in July 1936 the Fascist Minister of Education decreed the abolition of all official Montessori activities in Italy. Governments that desire to raise up a population of soldiers cannot afford to tolerate a system of education designed to produce free, intelligent and self-reliant individuals.

Ethics and War

Pacifism is the application of the principles of individual morality to the problems of politics and economics. In practice we have two systems of morality: one for individuals and another for communities. Behaviour which, in an individual, would be considered wrong is excused or even commended when indulged in by a national community. Men and women who would shrink from doing anything dishonourable in the sphere of personal relationships are ready to lie and swindle, to steal and even murder when they are representing their country. The community is regarded as a wholly immoral being and loyalty to the community serves to justify the individual in committing every kind of crime.

The wars of earlier days were relatively harmless affairs. Few conquerors were systematically destructive; Jinghiz Khan was an exceptional monster. To-day,

48

scientific weapons have made possible indiscriminate and unintentional destruction. Most military experts are agreed that a large-scale war waged with such weapons will be the ruin of European civilization. War was always wrong, and war-makers have always been men of criminal intentions; science has now provided the war-makers with the power of putting their intentions into destructive action on a scale which was undreamt of even a quarter of a century ago. In the past, national communities could afford to behave like maniacs or criminals. To-day the costs of lunacy and wickedness are excessive; nations can no longer afford to behave except like the sanest and most moral of beings.

Example

The advocates of a policy of unilateral disarmament believe that a genuinely pacifistic gesture by one of the great powers would profoundly affect public opinion throughout the world and would lead to a measure of general disarmament. Non-pacifists deny that such an example would be efficacious and insist that the only hope of security lies in the piling up of armaments and their pooling, if possible, for use by the League.

It is, of course, impossible exactly to forecast what would be the effect of unilateral disarmament by a great power, which could only be done in a democratic country with the consent of the majority of the electors. All that can be said is that, when the militarist denies the effectiveness of example, he is saying something which is completely belied by the facts of contemporary history.

49

By retaining their armaments after the World War, England and France set an example which was followed by all the lesser allied powers and, later, by Germany and the other countries which had been disarmed under the provisions of the Treaty of Versailles. The rapid rearmament of Germany has manifestly served as an example for the recent rapid increase in French and British armaments. All armament races are essentially the fruit of example. Under the pressure of fear, suspicion and desire for prestige, each competing nation feels bound to imitate the others. Gun is pitted against gun, plane against plane, poison bomb against poison bomb. In the end, one of the competitors finds that the strain is too great, and trusting in a momentary superiority, precipitates the catastrophe; or else there is an "incident"—a political assassination, such as that which served as pretext and occasion for the World War, a frontier skirmish, an insult to the flag; accidentally and against the conscious wishes of all concerned, the machinery of destruction is set in motion. The longer the competing nations have gone on following one another's example in piling up armaments, the more numerous and efficient will be the weapons of destruction and the more disastrous, in consequence, the effects of the conflict.

As already shown, each government explains the piling up of armaments as a precaution of "defence" against an aggressor. A disarmed nation could not conceivably be accused of being an aggressor. Complete disarmament would therefore mean absolute security.

We see then that example is enormously potent in the matter of armament. There is no reason to suppose that it will not be equally potent in the matter of disarmament. An act of unilateral disarmament would relieve international tension, allay fear and suspicion, calm the susceptibilities of those who feel that their prestige demands an army, navy or air force as big as the other fellow's. There is every reason to believe that a lead towards sanity would be followed. At present we prefer to give a lead towards insanity.

Unilateral disarmament by our country is the natural and consequential public policy which follows from the individual pledge of war resistance.

Force

Pacifism is often opposed on the ground that "civilization is based on force," "there cannot be justice unless it is imposed by force," and so on. What exactly does this word "force" stand for? The answer is that, when used in reference to human relations, it has no single definite meaning. "Force" is used by parents, when, without resort to any kind of physical compulsion, they make their children obey them. "Force" is used by the attendants in an asylum, when they restrain a maniac from hurting himself or others. "Force" is used by the police when they control traffic and "force" of another kind and in greater quantity is used by them when they make a baton charge. Finally, there is the "force" that is used in war. This varies with the mentality of the combatants and the weapons and other technical devices at their disposal. Chivalry has disappeared and the "rules of war" are coming to be ignored; in any future war "force" will probably mean violence and fraud used to the extreme limit of the belligerents' capacity.

"Force" used by armies making use of modern weapons is morally unjustifiable and is not even likely to secure its object, for the simple reason that these weapons are so destructive that a war cannot now preserve any of a nation's vital interests; it can only bring ruin and death indiscriminately to all who come within its range, innocent and guilty, attacker and attacked, soldier and civilian alike. Merely in order to be effective, "force" must be used in moderation.

Experience shows that the forces which accomplish most are psychological forces—the force of persuasion, the force of loyalty, the force of social tradition, the force of good example and the like.

Haves and Have-Nots

It is often said that the world is divided into two camps; that of the Haves and that of the Have-nots, that of the satiated nations, who want to keep what they already possess, and that of the dissatisfied nations, who want to increase their possessions. The mentality of the first group is summed up by the British Navy League poster, which represents a bulldog standing on a Union Jack with the caption: "What we have we hold." The mentality of the second group is expressed by the slogan which originated in Germany: "A place in the sun." It is worth noting that, of the twenty-five metals essential to the life of an industrial country, the British Empire has adequate supplies of eighteen, Japan of three, Germany of four, Italy of 4·3 (Dr. Alfred Salter, House of Commons, February 5, 1936).

Whether a colonial Empire is profitable to the colony-owning people as a whole is a question which economists find hard to decide. Certain English politicians have expressed the view that colonies do not pay. In spite of this, there are few indeed who are prepared to part with any colonial territory. But international politics are not framed on the basis of an exact accountancy. The question whether colonies pay or not is of secondary importance. The significant fact is that there is everywhere a great mass of opinion which thinks they pay and a still greater mass which associates national prestige with their possession. It may not be true that the sufferings of the Have-not nations are wholly or mainly due to their lack of colonies. But it probably is true that their peoples think that they are suffering for this reason; and it is certainly true that they regard the possession of colonies as a source of national prestige. A pacifism which consists in preserving the *status quo*, in "holding what we have," is not calculated to inspire much respect. "The implication is that England and America are the only two solvent nations in the Western world and that, since they have what they want and need, it is in their interest to preach peace (from *A Critique of Pacifism*, by Reinhold Niebuhr).

A policy of free trade on the part of the Haves can do something to mitigate the resentment of the Have-nots. Mr. Ramsay Muir has pointed out that "between 1850 and 1900 the whole of Africa was partitioned and we got the lion's share. How was it that the world allowed us to get it almost without any kind of struggle?

53

It was because the world knew that, if somebody else got it, the world would be excluded by tariffs, but that any territory acquired by Great Britain would be open to traders of other countries on equal terms with British traders." To-day, Mr. Ramsay Muir goes on to point out, "Great Britain has reversed that policy by the Ottawa agreement."

The resentment of the Have-nots against the Haves is likely to persist as long as the exclusive ownership of colonies persists. There can be no final solution to the problem until all colonial territories are either liberated and given their independence, or, if their peoples are really incapable of governing themselves under modern conditions, placed under the guardianship of a genuinely international body, to be administered for the benefit, first, of the inhabitants, and, second, of the world at large. (See *Economic Warfare; Imperialism and Colonies; Mandates*.)

Imperialism and Colonies

"Imperialism" is a word used in two senses. As a political principle it is often opposed to nationalism. Nationalism concentrates on the development of each nation. Imperialism concentrates on the advantage of one nation ruling over, guiding, and developing a number of other nations. The advantage claimed is that much greater political units are created under a single government. The disadvantage is that such a principle is generally accompanied by pride in mere size and grandeur, belief in the use of force, belief in the superiority of one

race over others, and a habit of boasting of one's strength
—all the things that are crystallized in the word "jingo."

The word "Imperialism" is more commonly used to
denote the actual system of empires as it now prevails.
Out of the sixty odd sovereign States of the world, only
six possess considerable empires—Great Britain, France,
Belgium, Portugal, Holland, Italy. These empires were
acquired for a variety of reasons—as a source of raw
materials, as an outlet for surplus population and surplus
production, as a source of profit to a small class of speculative financiers. It is doubtful whether colonies are
profitable to the colony-owning country as a whole.
To certain classes, however, such as financiers and
colonial administrators, they are profitable; and, since
these classes rule, there is a tendency for their interest
to be regarded as a national interest. Moreover, the
conception of prestige makes it hard for a nation to
abandon even a demonstrably useless possession.

In an empire, the idea of sovereignty and possession,
appropriate only to national states, has been extended
to vast groupings of subject or semi-subject peoples. In
the economic sphere, these great units have become more
and more exclusive.

The advantage of this exclusiveness to the people of
the mother country is highly questionable. It cannot
be disputed, however, that in a world of economic nationalism, the closing of markets, etc., to all but the citizens
of the mother country inflicts injury on the states which
do not possess empires.

It is claimed by the imperial or colonial powers that
they have prevented local wars, and advanced civilization
among backward peoples. It is claimed, on the other

55

side, that the advances in civilization have been far smaller than might have been achieved by a more disinterested form of government; and that the rivalries between the imperial, or would-be imperial powers, have been made far more serious by the exclusive empire system. All the wars of the past half-century, at least, have arisen out of conflicts between empires as to the control of various under-developed or "backward" portions of the world.

Imperialism is challenged from two sides. On the one hand, there is a rising tide of nationalism within the various empires, entailing demands for self-government and independence. On the other hand, there is an increasing realization that the whole idea of the exclusive empire belongs to an age that is past; and that the backward regions of the world, both in respect of economic development and cultural advance, should be regarded as a responsibility resting upon the international community as a whole. (See *Mandates; Defence; British Empire, The.*)

India, Pacifism in

Pre-Aryan India seems to have been a pacific country. The excavations at Mohenjo-Daro and Harappa have revealed no fortifications and very few weapons. At the same time there is evidence that the Yogic practices, which have played and still play so important a part in all Indian religions, had been developed as early as the fourth millennium B.C. The theology underlying such practices is a theology of immanence, which affirms that

56

the soul of the individual is a portion of the divine soul of the world. Yogic practices are designed to make the individual become conscious of this identity between his inmost self and the spirit of the universe. This theology is summed up in the phrase: "Thou art that." Pacifism and humanitarianism are the necessary corollaries of this doctrine. The Hinduism of historical times is a religion combining elements of widely different value. For those who want such things, it provides magic and orgiastic fertility rites; for the more spiritual it provides mysticism and a high philosophy. Its caste system is a kind of static militarism, in which the position of conquerors and conquered has been petrified into an unchanging social order. The doctrine that "thou art that," with its accompanying mystical practices and its humanitarian consequences, has persisted as a standing protest against this fossilized militarism.

Humanitarian and pacifist principles were proclaimed and acted upon, often with excessive scrupulousness, by the followers of Jainisen, a dissident sect of Hinduism which came into existence in the sixth and fifth centuries B.C.

More important was the rise of Buddhism at about the same period. Like the Jains, the Buddhists taught and practised *ahimsa*, or harmlessness, refraining from doing hurt to any living being. Even Buddhist laymen were expected to refuse to have anything to do with the manufacture and sale of arms, with the making of poisons or strong drink, with soldiering or the slaughter of animals. Buddhism is the only great world religion which has made its way without bloodshed or persecution, without censorship or inquisition. It is interesting to compare Buddhist and Christian views on anger. For Buddhism anger is always and unconditionally wrong and disgraceful. For Christians, in whose bible the savage literature of the ancient Hebrews is included on the same footing as the prophetic writing and the New Testament, anger may be a divine attribute. What is called "righteous indignation" has justified Christian churchmen in committing innumerable atrocities. (See *China, Pacifism in; Christ, The Teaching of.*)

Individual Disputes and National Disputes

There is a fundamental difference between war and disputes between individuals. Individuals quarrel in hot blood; war is coolly and scientifically prepared in advance and soldiers are carefully trained in order that they may overcome their natural feelings and be ready to kill and to be killed at the word of command.

Individuals fight in their own quarrels; soldiers are trained to fight in quarrels that are not their own—for the financial advantage of business interests, for national prestige, for the sake of potential military advantages. (It is worthy of note that one of the causes of war is war itself. Wars are fought in order that the victor may have a better strategic position during future wars. The possession of an army and navy is in itself a reason for going to war; "we must use our forces now," so runs the argument, "in order that we may be in a position to use them to better advantage another time.")

58

In some cases individuals fight in self-defence against a bully or a criminal. This fact provides the militarist with a favourite argument. "If an individual policeman is justified in arresting an individual criminal, a national policeman is justified in arresting a national criminal." The analogy is entirely false. The individual policeman arrests one man—the man who is guilty. The national policeman (represented by an army, navy and air force) uses all the means at his disposal—and these means are now diabolically effective—not to arrest one guilty person, but to destroy, maim, starve and ruin millions of men, women and children, the overwhelming majority of whom have committed no crime of any sort. The process which righteous militarists describe as "punishing a guilty nation" consists in mangling and murdering innumerable innocent individuals. To draw analogies between an army and a policeman, between war (however "righteous" its aims) and the prevention of crime, is utterly misleading.

Another favourite question asked by militarists is the following: "What would you do if you saw a stranger break into your house and try to violate your wife?" This question may be answered as follows: "Whatever else I might do—and it is quite likely that I should become very angry and try to knock the intruder down or even to kill him—I should certainly not send my brother to go and poison the man's grandfather and disembowel his infant son." And that precisely is what war consists of—murdering, either personally or (more often) through the instrumentality of others, all kinds of people who have never done one any sort of injury.

International Police Force

This proposal either takes the form of a complete international force of navy and army and air force, as advocated by the New Commonwealth, or an international air police force, officially supported by the Labour Party. It is argued that instead of depending in an emergency on doubtful military contributions from various nations, a standing force under the direction of the League of Nations should be established. But apart from the doubt as to whether a declared aggressor can be thwarted and forced into acquiescence by methods of violence, there would be insuperable difficulties in enlisting, recruiting, arming, training and even locating such an armed body, and its command and release for action would require a unanimous international decision which would not be likely to be forthcoming. In the world of to-day it is inconceivable that French and Germans, Russians and Italians, Americans and Japanese would unite together in order to man such a force; it is inconceivable that the staff officers of the various nations would draw up in advance elaborate plans of campaign for an attack, in certain contingencies, on their own countries. If certain nations refused to participate the main purpose would not be served and if the contribution in men of any one nation or combination of nations preponderated they would be accused of trying to dominate the world.

The proposal is not only undesirable but utterly impracticable. (See *Sanctions*.)

International Politics in the Light of Christ's Teaching

It has generally been taken for granted that Jesus regarded political affairs as entirely outside His orbit. There is reason, however, to believe that this view is erroneous.

(1) The stories of the Baptism, the Temptation, the conversation at Caesarea-Philippi, the trials before Caiaphas and Pilate, and the entry into Jerusalem, make it certain that Jesus regarded Himself as Messiah. Now, all conceptions of Messiahship had this in common: the Messiah was essentially a national figure. Questioned by Pilate, Jesus avows Himself King of *the Jews*.

(2) At the beginning of His ministry, Jesus expected that His messianic plan for Israel would be successful, as is clear from the fact towards the end (see Matt. xxiii. 37 ff.; Luke xiii. 34 f.; xix. 41 ff.). He expressed his disappointment that the Jews had refused to follow Him as leader. As "King of the Jews," what did Jesus have in mind for His people?

(3) Release from foreign domination was the great political preoccupation of the Jewish contemporaries of Jesus. All of them believed that the Gentiles would be overthrown and destroyed, enslaved or, in a few cases, converted, by divine power in the course of a great messianic war. Jesus must have had something to say on this question. His conception of the Messiah's function was, however, very different from theirs. His plan for the Jews seems to have been that, under His leadership, they should give up their desire for vengeance

61

against Rome and for the destruction of the Gentiles and that, trusting wholly to deeds of love, should undercut Gentile hostility by means of "non-violence" and convert enemies to friends, uniting them in the brotherhood of true religion. The Jews, in a word, were to be the pioneers of a new kind of religio-political action.

(4) In support of this contention, it may be pointed out that the injunction in the Sermon on the Mount of love for enemies does not, as has been generally supposed, refer exclusively to individual conduct in the private relationship of life. "Whoever shall compel thee" (Matt. v. 41) seems to be a reference to the forced labour imposed by Roman and Herodian officials. The word for "enemies" is perfectly general and may refer equally well to public and private enemies. The word "neighbour" is a technical term for "fellow-Israelite" (cf. Lev. xix. 18) and the exhortation to love not neighbours only is therefore an exhortation to love Gentiles. In Luke xii. 54–xiii. 9, Jesus seems to be urging the need for reconciliation with the enemy before it is too late and to be pointing out that, unless His countrymen repent and give up their ideas of violent revolt and vengeance, they will assuredly be destroyed. The lamentation over Jerusalem (Luke xix. 41–4) and the words to the woman on the road to Golgotha (Luke xxiii. 27–31) convey the same idea. The advice that Cæsar's tribute should be submissively paid is in line with the whole scheme of effecting a reconciliation between Israel and Rome.

The fall of Jerusalem in A.D. 70 followed the Jewish rejection of Jesus and His policy—followed it in virtue of an inexorable psychological law: Acts of love beget love: acts of hatred beget hatred. To the policy of

Jesus the Jews preferred armed revolt; the Romans reacted against violence with violence, and, since they were the stronger, Jerusalem was sacked, even as Jesus had predicted. "If thou hadst known the things that belong unto thy peace! but now they are hid from thine eyes." Because these things were hid, because the eyes of the Jews were closed, Jerusalem suffered destruction.

(See *The Politics of Jesus*, by C. J. Cadoux, in *Congregational Quarterly*, Jan. 1936, pp. 58–67.)

League of Nations

Many rested their hopes on the establishment of an international body for the settlement of disputes as the one good feature which might emerge from the devastating conflict of the Great War. President Wilson took a leading part and the Covenant of the League of Nations was drawn up and, very unfortunately, attached as part of the Treaty of Versailles, in 1919. President Wilson was thrown over by his own people and the U.S.A. never joined the League. The co-called enemy countries, Germany, Austria, Bulgaria and Turkey, were not admitted till some years later. Germany was not invited to enter the League till 1926. The League therefore has never been complete. Soviet Russia eventually joined. But Japan withdrew in March 1933 and Germany withdrew in October 1933. The suspicion that the League had been affixed to the Treaty of Versailles in order to maintain the *status quo* as laid down by the punitive clauses in the Treaty, was not without justification.

63

The League has done good work in subsidiary matters and its constructive work might well be strengthened. It has also resolved minor international disputes. But the great error of its founders in proposing the use of collective force as a method of preventing or stopping aggressive warfare on the part of any one of the Great Powers has been demonstrated in the cases of Japan and Italy. The attempt to carry out this provision has greatly weakened the authority of the League. Until the League is all-inclusive and the obligation to use force in any circumstance is eliminated from the Covenant, its continued existence may be regarded as doubtful. If some nations adhere to the Covenant while others remain outside, the result can only be the establishment of two hostile camps.

(Consult *The Aims and Organization of the League of Nations* (published by the Secretariat of the League). On the reform of the League, see L. P. Jacks, *A Demilitarized League of Nations* (*Hibbert Journal*, Aug. 1936).

Liberty

War is incompatible with liberty. So, to a lesser extent, is intensive preparation for war. Conscription, or military slavery, is universal on the Continent of Europe. In the dictatorial states, Italy, Germany and Russia, even children are taught rifle drill and the use of the machine-gun.

Thanks to their country's geographical position, Englishmen have hitherto avoided military slavery. Navies can be manned with a comparatively small force and, except during the Great War, when conscription was temporarily introduced, England has had no need of a large army.

There are signs that this state of things may soon be changed, and that Englishmen and perhaps also English women and children will soon be subjected to some form of military slavery. This military slavery will probably not take the form of continental conscription. The rise of air power has made it very doubtful whether huge national armies will ever be used again. But at the same time air power has made it certain that the whole civilian population will be involved in any future war as it never was involved in the past. What the militarist fears above everything is that an untrained civilian population will rapidly lose its "will-to-war," if subjected to prolonged bombardment from the air. Therefore, he argues, civilians must be disciplined to endure the horrors of war, even as soldiers are disciplined. In this way and in this way only will it be possible for the military machine to score a "victory" over the military machine of the enemy. Whether this "victory" will be worth having is a matter which the militarist refuses to consider. He wants to win and he does not mind whether half the population and all the decencies of civilized life are sacrificed in the process.

In the dictatorial countries not only the young men of military age, but all civilians without exception, are subjected to military training in the form of gas drill, practice black-outs and evacuations, periodical parades, etc. There is every indication that our militarists will soon demand that similar measures should be put into force in this country. Gas drills may seem harmless enough; indeed, attempts will be made to represent them as genuine defence measures. In reality, as has been shown in the article on Defence, gas drills, black-outs and the like, are almost completely futile as defence. The military experts know that they are useless, but desire to impose them, first, because gas drills may create a consoling illusion of security and, second, because they offer a golden opportunity for imposing military control on the civil population. The truth is that these seemingly harmless exercises are only the first instalment of complete military slavery.

The militarist's ideal is a country that is one vast barrack, inhabited by well-drilled men, women and children, prepared at the word of command to "do or die" (especially to die) without ever attempting to "reason why." In the words of Mr. Jonathan Griffin, air-power threatens to "make liberty a thing of the past, and reduce the whole of Europe to the condition of those parts of it which in the 'Dark Ages' were really dark."

Mandates

The Mandate System is clearly and conveniently described in Article XXII of the Covenant of the League of Nations. It came into being after the Great War as a means of dealing with parts of the Turkish Empire, and with the German colonies, which had been occupied by the Allies. It was a compromise between those who wished to annex these territories outright, and those who (like President Wilson) wanted to place them under something like international administration. What happened

66

was that the "Allied and Associated Powers" (a term which included the U.S.A.) allotted them to certain States—Great Britain, South Africa, Australia, New Zealand, France and (later) Belgium—as "mandated territories." These States were to exercise all the powers of governments, but subject to certain definite obligations to the League. They were to report annually to a Mandates Commission, consisting of persons chosen for their expert knowledge, but not officially representing particular Governments; the Mandates Commission being responsible to the Council of the League of Nations. They were also to fulfil the conditions laid down in Article XXII and in the separate Mandates of each territory. The chief conditions are:

(a) equality of economic opportunity for all League of Nations members;

(b) no fortifications or bases, or military training of Natives for other than police purposes and the defence of territory;

(c) justice to Natives;

(d) freedom of conscience and religion;

(e) prohibition of abuses.

The Mandates Commission has no power of enforcing its decisions, but in fact its powers of inquiry and of securing world publicity have done something to raise the standard of administration and to promote the idea of international responsibility for the "backward" areas of the world. It seems clear that the Mandate System can and should be developed. (See *Imperialism and Colonies; British Empire, The; Defence.*)

67

Mineral Sanctions

"Mineral Sanctions" were first proposed by Sir Thomas Holland, F.R.S., in his presidential address to the British Association in 1929. The theme was more fully developed in a small book (*The Mineral Sanction*) by the same author, published in 1935.

What follows is a brief summary of the main points in the scheme.

(1) No country is self-sufficient in regard to supplies of minerals.

(2) Minerals cannot be made artificially, nor can they be replaced by synthetic substitutes.

(3) No industrialized country can carry on without a steady and sufficient supply of minerals. In war-time the normal supply must be increased by anything from five to twenty times.

(4) Seeing that all countries are dependent upon others for supplies of certain indispensable minerals, it follows that an international agreement to refuse to sell minerals to a belligerent would be an effective method of stopping or at least shortening a war.

Let us consider a few concrete examples.

Great Britain is mainly or entirely dependent on oversea sources for supplies of copper, chrome, lead, zinc, sulphur, mercury, tungsten, nickel, molybdenum, mica, manganese, cobalt, antimony and bauxite (for the extraction of aluminium).

Germany has no bauxite, no antimony, no chrome, insufficient copper and iron, almost no manganese, no mica, no molybdenum, no mercury, hardly any nickel, sulphur, tin or tungsten.

68

France depends wholly on foreign sources for chrome, copper, manganese, mercury, mica, molybdenum, nickel, sulphur, tin and tungsten. She is partly dependent on foreign countries for zinc, lead, coal and antimony.

Both Japan and Italy are even poorer in indispensable minerals than the countries listed above. Even the United States, by far the richest in natural resources of all the great powers, is not self-sufficient where minerals are concerned. The same is true of Russia which, though more plentifully supplied than her neighbours to East and West, has to depend on foreign sources for supplies of antimony, copper, molybdenum, nickel, quicksilver, sulphur, tin and tungsten.

To anyone who considers these facts it must be sufficiently clear that a system of mineral sanctions offers very good prospects for shortening hostilities, when once they have broken out, and even for controlling the preparations for future wars. No attempt, however, has been made to establish such a system. The rulers of the nations prefer to carry on the traditional policy, which is to arm their own people and at the same time to sell to their neighbours the minerals which, in all probability, will be used against the sellers in the form of armaments.

Moral Equivalent of War

A common defence of war is that it is a school of virtues. In war a man learns obedience, courage, self-sacrifice; he throws away his life that a greater purpose may triumph. It is true that war may evoke these virtues. But we must not forget that it also evokes and encourages a

69

number of vices. In war, the actual fighters learn to be inhuman and cruel, while the politicians who direct the fighters learn to lie and swindle. For the behaviour of politicians, the reader is referred to the articles *Propaganda* and *Secret Treaties*. As for the fighters, these were actually subjected during the World War to a systematic education in cruelty. Lectures on bayonet fighting were intended to heighten the bloodthirstiness of recruits. The following citation is from a military manual for use in the American Army. (The paragraph, which has now been modified, was cited in *The World To-morrow*, New York, Feb. 1926). "Bayonet fighting is possible only because red-blooded men naturally possess the fighting instinct. This inherent desire to fight and kill must be carefully watched for and encouraged by the instructor. To finish an opponent who hangs on, or attempts to pull you to the ground, always try to break his hold by driving the knee or foot to his crotch and gouging his eyes with your thumbs. Men still have fight in them unless you hit a vital spot. But when the bayonet comes out and the air sucks in, and they begin to bleed on the inside, they feel the pain and lose their fight."

It will be seen, then, that the military virtues have to be paid for, and paid for pretty highly. But the virtues, let us admit frankly, exist. If civil life does not evoke these virtues, then we must change civil life until it does. Otherwise war can still defend itself by being able to claim (if not actually to prove) that it is more moral than peace.

What, then, is the moral equivalent of war? It is a way of living which calls out endurance, bravery and self-forgetfulness, but for constructive ends and not for

70

destruction. In war, a man is asked to lay down his life in defence of his country, and his natural devotion responds, and responds gladly in many cases, to that call. His sacrifice is admirable; but the accompaniments of that sacrifice and the reasons for which it is made are far from admirable. For what he is being asked to do is to go on killing other men until such time as he himself is killed by them. And when we ask for what purpose he is to kill and be killed, we find as often as not that the war is being fought for the most ignoble reasons. In all war there is a most unsatisfactory mixture of private virtue with public and private vice. Yet so strong in men is the wish to serve a cause greater than themselves and to lose themselves in that cause, and so incapable are our peace-time societies of giving us that sense of being wanted by a great and noble cause, that it is easy to persuade men to take part in war. All they wish to do is to show their devotion and courage; what they actually succeed in doing is to participate in an orgy of mass murder, a campaign against civilization.

Modern dictatorships owe much of their popularity, not to their successful campaigns abroad, but to the fact that they have been able to make so many of their peoples believe that by disciplined effort and sacrifice they could, all together, build up a united nation freed from poverty and class selfishness.

Beside the desire for discipline and self-sacrifice, there is also in healthy people, especially when they are young, a love of risk and a need to live dangerously. Our societies are not only too meaningless; they are also, for many people, too safe, too unexciting. Hard games get rid of some of this pent energy; but games are inadequate. War

71

still attracts men because they want to risk their lives and not merely keep themselves fit. A system of peace-time national service should be organized, making it possible for every boy and young man to take his turn at one or other of the tough jobs and civilian risks that exist—fire-brigade service, life-boat service, light-house service, sea fishery, mine safety work, down to traffic direction and sewer inspection. Those whose physique would not permit such roughing could gain as much honour by offering themselves for essential scientific experiments. In some such way as this individuals would be given a cause to live for and if necessary to die for—would be enabled to practise the soldier's virtues without committing the crime of war.

Morality of Pacifism

It is often objected that pacifism is morally unjustifiable. "Your position in society," the critic of pacifism argues, "is that of a parasite. You are profiting by what the armed forces of your country are doing to preserve you and your family from danger but you refuse to undertake defence work yourself and you try to persuade others to follow your example. You have no right to take from the society in which you live without giving anything in return."

Several answers to these criticisms present themselves:

(1) In the contemporary world, the armed forces of a country do not provide its inhabitants with protection. On the contrary, their existence is one of the principal sources of national danger. There is no more effective

way of provoking people to attack than to threaten them. At the present time Great Britain combines extreme vulnerability with formidable aggressive armament. Our policy of rearmament with weapons of aggression is one which positively invites attack. The pacifist is criticized as a shirker who seeks security behind a line of soldiers, sailors and airmen, whom he refuses to help. In reality, his dearest wish is to get rid of the soldiers, sailors and airmen, and all their machinery of destruction; for he knows that so long as they are there, security will be unattainable. Tanks, bombers and battleships do not give security; on the contrary, they are a constant source of danger.

(2) Those who accuse pacifists of being parasites upon the society in which they live should pause for a moment to consider a few facts and figures. Since the last war this country has spent sixteen hundred millions of pounds upon its armaments, and the rate of expenditure is now to be increased. The world as a whole spends nearly two thousand millions a year on its "defence forces." These "defence forces" live at the expense of the working community, performing no constructive work, absorbing an increasing amount of the world's energy and not only failing to provide the individual citizens of the various nations with adequate protection, but actually inviting attack from abroad. To the inhabitant of a bombarded London it will be no satisfaction to learn that the planes for which he has been paying so heavily in taxation are bombarding some foreign capital.

(3) Refusal to obey the government of the society of which one is a member is a very serious matter. Still, most moralists and political philosophers have been of

73

opinion that individuals are fully justified in disobeying the State if the State commands them to do something which they are convinced to be wrong. Social solidarity is not always desirable. There is such a thing as solidarity with evil as well as solidarity with good. A man who finds himself on a pirate ship is morally justified in refusing to co-operate with his shipmates in their nefarious activities. All reformers have been men who refused to co-operate, on some important issue, with the societies of which they were members. That is why so many of them have been persecuted by their contemporaries. The Christian religion takes its name from a persecuted reformer.

Criticisms and answers:

(1) The State provides free schools, libraries, pensions, etc. In return the individual should do what the State demands of him.

Answer: (a) The individual pays for State services in taxation.

(b) The State is not God and its demands are not categorical imperatives. The State was made for man, not man for the State. The State is a convenience, like drains or the telephone; its demand that it should be treated as an all-wise divinity is inadmissible and leads, as the history of tyrannies and dictatorships shows, to every kind of crime and disaster.

(c) If the State may justifiably demand of an individual that he should commit murder for the sake of his country, then it is equally justified in demanding that he should commit lesser crimes. But we can imagine the outcry that would be raised by pious militarists if, for example, in an effort to raise the birth-rate and improve the quality

74

of the race, the State were to conscribe all women and compel them to have sexual intercourse with eugenically selected men.

(2) "The pacifist method of dealing with war is too slow and there will be another war before there are enough pacifists to stop it."

The pacifist method is certainly slow; but the militarist's method is far slower. Indeed, the militarist's method is foredoomed to make no advance whatever towards the goal of peace. War produces more war. Only non-violence can produce non-violence. Pacifism is admittedly slow and hard to practise; but the fact remains that it is the only method of getting universal peace which promises to be in the least effective.

(3) "There is something worse than war, and that is injustice." But war inevitably commits injustices far greater and more widespread than those it was called upon to redress.

(4) "Pacifism tends to increase the arrogance and power of dictators."

(a) None of the modern dictators has been faced with large-scale pacifism. Where non-violence has been used on a large scale (see *Non-Violence*) even violent and ruthless rulers have been nonplussed.

(b) What increases the arrogance of dictators is not so much pacifism as the half-hearted use of their own violent methods. The violence of dictators must be opposed either by violence greater than theirs (with the certainty of prolonging the war habit and the possibility of doing irreparable damage to civilization) or else by complete pacifism (which, however slow and difficult, will ultimately lead to the establishment of peace).

75

Nationalism

We cannot discuss nationalism without first defining the word "nation," and the only definition which covers the ground is "a community organized for war."

It is clear that a nation is not a racial entity, since many millions of Negroes are nationals of the United States; it is not a linguistic entity, since the Swiss nation is composed of speakers of German, French and Italian; it is not even a geographical entity, since the German nation is cut in two by Poland, and the Swiss Canton of Ticino is geographically as well as linguistically part of Italy.

The definition given above is that recognized by the League of Nations, which admits to membership a community, however small, which has an army of its own, but refuses admission to a community, however large, whose autonomous powers do not include the provision of armed forces.

California is not now entitled to membership; but if a revolution were to divide it among a dozen bloodthirsty dictators, each of these could be represented at Geneva.

A nationalist is thus a person who wishes to surround himself, and those who can be induced to conspire with him, with a closely and aggressively guarded military frontier, and incidentally to prevent as far as possible that cross-fertilization of ideas which always has been and always must be the sole insurance against the relapse into barbarism which perpetually threatens all human communities.

Nationalistic Religion

During the last hundred years Europe has witnessed a rapid and accelerating movement away from monotheism towards tribal idolatry. The place of God has been largely usurped by such deified entities as the Nation, the Race, the Class, the Party. In the totalitarian states these abstract entities are embodied in the person of a semi-divine Leader. (We are reminded of the king-worship imposed upon their subjects by the successors of Alexander the Great, of that Roman emperor-worship in which the early Christians steadfastly refused to participate.)

In every country, liberal as well as totalitarian, the local idolatry is preached in schools, in the press, over the wireless, in political speeches, very often even from Christian pulpits. In dictatorial countries this preaching is more systematic and probably more effective than in liberal countries; that is all. The dictators aim at inspiring young people with a crusading enthusiasm for the local idol and his deified vice-regent. They are trying to do what was done in the seventies of last century by the makers of modern Japan. These astute psychologists took the ancient religion of Japan, Shintoism, and adapted it for use in a modern, centralized state. The Emperor became God, and the first duty of his subjects was to live and work and, if necessary, die for the God-Emperor and his accredited representatives. "A new system of compulsory education was introduced to inculcate before all worldly knowledge the duty of unconditional obedience to the Son of Heaven, the Mikado, whose service is perfect freedom." The makers of new

Japan had this advantage over the contemporary dictators: Shintoism was an existing religion with traditionally hallowed rites and beliefs. The dictators of modern Europe have to create their equivalents of Shintoism. The traditional religion of Europe is not nationalism; it is Christianity in one or other of its forms.

The churches have protested against the idolatrous deification of the State, but without much effect. For the present generation, the claim of the churches to stand for the brotherhood of man in the fatherhood of God was seriously compromised during the last war. In 1914 the ecclesiastical authorities in all the belligerent countries enthusiastically threw in their lot with their respective governments and preached a holy war against fellow Christians, merely because they happened to be living on the wrong side of the national frontier. (In a service of intercession, sanctioned by the Archbishop of Canterbury in September 1914, we find the following sentence: "We pray thee, O God, to judge between us and the enemy, and of Thy great mercy to give us the victory.")

Psychologically speaking, the strength of nationalistic idolatry lies in its power to assuage the sense of personal inferiority. Here, for example, is an individual who is poor, exploited, socially insignificant; to him come the apostles of the local idolatry, assuring him that, as a member of the divine Nation, Party, Class or Race, he is superior to everyone else in the world outside his own particular community. The nation-god is glorious and even his feeblest and most unimportant worshippers mystically participate in that glory.

Nationalistic idolatry inculcates pride and vanity, on

78

the one hand, and hatred and contempt for foreigners on the other. It is essentially a religion of war. Pacifists should make it their business to understand the nature of this evil religion and, having understood it, to steel their minds against the emotional appeals and lying suggestions which are incessantly being made in its name.

Non-Violence

Pacifists believe—and their belief is based upon individual experience and a study of history, past and contemporary—that the most effective, the most equitable, the most economical way of meeting violence is to use non-violence.

If violence is answered by violence, the result is a physical struggle. Now, a physical struggle inevitably arouses hatred, fear, rage and resentment. In the heat of passion all scruples are thrown to the winds, all the habits of forbearance and humaneness acquired during years of civilized living are forgotten. Nothing matters any more except victory. And when at last victory comes to one or other of the parties, this final outcome of physical struggle bears no relation to the rights or wrongs of the case; nor, in most instances, does it provide any lasting settlement to the dispute at issue. (The cases in which victory does provide some kind of lasting settlement may be classified as follows: (1) Victory is final where the vanquished are completely or very nearly exterminated. In the case of war between two populous countries extermination is unlikely: one war tends therefore to beget another. (2) Victory may lead to an unquestioned settlement where the fighting forces involved are so small that the mass of the population is left unaffected by the struggle. To-day the entire population is liable to be affected by war. The relatively harmless wars conducted according to an elaborate code of rules by a small warrior-caste are things of the past. (3) Victory may lead to permanent peace where the victors settle down among the vanquished as a ruling minority and are, in due course, absorbed by them. This does not apply to contemporary wars. (4) Finally, victory may be followed by an act of reparation on the part of the victors to the vanquished. This will disarm resentment and lead to a genuine settlement. It was the policy pursued by the English after the Boer War. Such a policy is essentially an application of the principles of non-violence. The longer and the more savage the conflict, the more difficult is it to make an act of reparation after victory. It was relatively easy to be just after the Boer War; it was psychologically all but impossible to be just in 1918. That is why the pacifist insists that the principles of non-violence should be applied, wherever possible, before physical conflict has actually broken out.)

Non-violence does not mean doing nothing. It means making the enormous effort required to overcome evil with good. Non-violence does not rely on strong muscles and devilish armaments; it relies on moral courage, self-control and the knowledge, unswervingly acted upon, that there is in every human being, however brutal, however personally hostile, a fund of kindness, a love of justice, a respect for goodness and truth which can be reached by anyone who uses the right means.

80

To use these means is often extraordinarily hard; but history shows that it can be done—and done not only by exceptional individuals, but by large groups of ordinary men and women and even by governments.

In the paragraphs which follow, a few instances are cited, illustrating the way in which non-violence has been used, first, by isolated individuals, second, by groups and, thirdly, by governments.

During the American Civil War no consideration was shown to those who objected to war on religious grounds. After being cruelly tortured, Seth Loflin, a Quaker, was offered a gun. In spite of threats and abuse, he refused to take it; whereupon he was court-martialled, and condemned to be shot out of hand. In the presence of the firing squad Loflin, who was absolutely calm, asked time for prayer, saying, "Father, forgive them, for they know not what they do." The soldiers were so much impressed that they lowered their guns and, braving the penalty for disobedience, refused to shoot on such a man.

Dr. Theodore Pennell went to India in 1892, as a medical missionary. His work lay among the wild tribes on the North-West Frontier. Dressed as a Pathan and sharing the Pathans' mode of living, he travelled about the country unarmed and unafraid, giving his services to all who needed them. Hearing that a band of warriors had been ordered to take him alive or dead, Pennell made his way directly to the Mullah who had given the order. Astonished and deeply impressed by the doctor's courage, the Mullah gave him food, listened to his account of what he was doing and, when night came, ordered that his bed should be placed between his own and that of his son, thus indicating that the stranger was under his protection.

It is in the East that we find the most striking examples of non-violence practised by large groups. In South Africa and later in India, Gandhi organized non-violent resistance to the Government. The South African experiment was remarkably successful. In India a number of very considerable successes were recorded, and it was shown that very large groups of men and women could be trained to respond to the most brutal treatment with a quiet courage and equanimity that profoundly impressed their opponents, the spectators in the immediate vicinity and, through press accounts, the public opinion of the whole civilized world. The difficulty of effectively training very large numbers in a very short time proved too great. In a number of cases, inadequately trained groups resorted to mass violence. Rather than see his movement degenerate into civil war (in which, incidentally, the British, being better armed, would inevitably have won a complete victory) Gandhi called off his movement.

In 1919 a movement of non-violent resistance to Japanese imperialism broke out in Corea. In spite of the brutality of Japanese repression, the movement remained essentially pacifistic. Unfortunately for the Coreans, their leaders were not sufficiently practical. The boycotting of Japanese goods, civil disobedience, non-co-operation and refusal to pay taxes were not effectively organized on a large scale. These methods, which were used so effectively in India and again in China (where the shooting of unarmed students by the Shanghai police led, in 1925, to a formidable boycott of British goods), were tried out too late in Corea. The movement was only partially successful. The Japanese repressed it with savage violence, but were compelled to make very considerable concessions. At the same time the psychological effect of the movement upon the Coreans themselves was very great; as a people they recovered their self-respect and the revolt of 1919 was followed by a kind of renaissance of the best elements of Corean civilization.

Examples of non-violent acts by governments are seldom of a very heroic kind and the motives behind them are seldom unmixed. The tradition of politics is a thoroughly dishonourable one. The world sanctions a double system of morality—one system for private individuals, another for social groups. Men who, in private life, are consistently honest, humane and considerate, believe that when they act as representatives of a group, they are justified in doing things which, as individuals, they know to be utterly disgraceful.

During their working hours, the most high-minded politicians will practise deception and give orders for the murder of their fellows. To get rid of this odious tradition that, in politics and to some degree also in business, it may be one's duty to do what one knows to be wrong is one of the urgent tasks to which all pacifists should apply themselves. Meanwhile the tradition still persists; and it is for this reason that application of the principles of non-violence and even of plain morality by governments are so rare. At best the application is incomplete. In many cases it follows on an unsuccessful attempt to solve some thorny problem by means of violence. Such was the case, for example, in South Africa, when, as has been mentioned above,

83

Campbell-Bannerman gave the Boers self-government. The methods of violence had been tried, during the South African War, and found completely wanting. The war had solved no problems; it had merely created a number of new problems. Campbell Bannerman's courageous policy was crowned by a measure of success which it would have been utterly impossible to achieve by means of violent repression.

Something of the same sort happened in Ireland. After attempting, quite unsuccessfully, to compel the Irish to be loyal subjects to the Crown, the English suddenly reversed their policy and granted Home Rule. The result was, not indeed enthusiastic co-operation (after centuries of oppression, that would have been too much to expect), but at any rate peace. It did at least become possible for the English to get rid of the national disgrace of the Black-and-Tans.

In recent European history, the most complete examples of the application of non-violent principles by governments are supplied by Sweden and Norway. In 1814 the Treaty of Kiel provided that Norway should be handed over to the kingdom of Sweden. Bernadotte invaded the country; but after a fortnight, during which no serious conflict took place, opened negotiations. The union of the two countries was agreed upon, being achieved, in the words of the preamble to the Act of Union, "not by force of arms, but by free conviction." Ninety years later, in 1905, the union was dissolved. By an overwhelming majority, the Norwegians decided to become independent. The Swedes accepted that decision. No violence was used on either side. (See *Force; Revolution.*)

84

Over-Population and Food Supply

Preparations for aggressive and imperialistic wars are often excused on the ground of over-population. Rulers of countries preparing for war point out that the domestic food supply is insufficient and that their peoples must either acquire new territory or starve.

Now, much of the difficulty experienced by certain countries in securing adequate food supplies is due predominantly to a faulty monetary policy, which prevents them from buying from abroad. This faulty monetary policy is due in its turn to the determination of the governments of the countries concerned to spend all available national resources on armaments. Food cannot be bought because the country is preparing to go to war; the country must go to war because food cannot be bought. As usual, it is a vicious circle.

Faulty monetary policy may prevent certain nations from buying food abroad. But even if the policy were altered, it would still remain true that food would have to be obtained from abroad. In relation to home supplies, certain countries (including Germany, Japan and Great Britain) may be described as over-populated. To what extent is this over-population a valid excuse for new aggression or the continuance of long-established imperialism? According to experts trained in the techniques of modern agro-biology, imperialism has now lost its principal justification. Readers are referred to Dr. Willcox's book, *Nations Can Live at Home*, for a systematic exposition of the agro-biologist's case. For pacifists, the significant fact is this: any country which chooses to apply the most advanced agro-biological methods to the

85

growing of food-plants, including grasses for live-stock, can support a population far in excess of the densest population existing anywhere on the earth's surface at the present time. (The methods advocated by Dr. Willcox have already been used commercially on a large scale. The revolutionary system of "dirtless farming" devised by Professor Gericke of California is still in the experimental stage; but if it turns out to be satisfactory, it promises a more copious supply of food, produced with less labour and on a smaller area, than any other method can offer.)

It is profoundly significant that no government has hitherto made any serious effort to apply modern agrobiological methods for the purpose of raising the standard of well-being among its subjects and of rendering imperialism superfluous. As has been pointed out elsewhere in this book, the causes of war are psychological as well as economic. People prepare for war, among other reasons, because war is in the great tradition; because their education has left them militaristically minded; because they live in a society where success is worshipped and competition is more highly appreciated than cooperation; because war is exciting and gives them certain personal or vicarious satisfactions. Hence the reluctance to embark on such constructive policies as mineral sanctions or intensive agriculture—policies which show some genuine promise of stopping war or removing its causes. Hence, too, the extraordinary energy which governments and peoples put into such destructive, war-provoking policies as rearmament, centralization and the enslavement of individuals to the state. Practical pacifists should work for any constructive policy which offers some hope of removing the causes of conflict. Among

86

such policies, that of improving the methods of agriculture takes an important place.

Patriotism

"Patriotism," in Nurse Cavell's words, "is not enough."

It is not enough for the same reason as fetishism is not enough—because there is a larger Whole of which one's own country is only a small part. To give to an isolated part of the universe that reverence which properly belongs only to the Whole (or in the words of religion, to God) is idolatry; and idolatry is not only philosophically absurd, it is also disastrous in practice. The worship of a part as though it were the Whole provokes strife with the worshippers of other isolated parts. Each system of idolatry encourages its adherents to hate the adherents of all other systems.

In the case of patriotism we see that an idolatrous love of one's country is always accompanied by dislike and contempt of other people's countries. Where the nation is regarded as being in some sort a God, men feel that they have an excuse for indulging in pride and vanity in regard to themselves and their own people, and scorn and dislike in regard to the members of other nations. Hellenes and Barbarians, Chosen People and Gentiles, Aryans and Non-Aryans, Proletarians and Bourgeois, God's Englishmen and "The Lesser Breeds without the Law"—the words expressing self-praise and contempt for others have varied from age to age and from country to country; but the disgraceful sentiments of idolatrous patriotism have always been the same.

To get rid of patriotism altogether is neither possible nor even desirable. Every human individual is born into one particular society and brought up to speak one particular language. His habits of thought and feelings are shaped in the moulds of one particular national tradition. It is inevitable that he should feel a special devotion for the community of which he is a member. Moreover, the fact that he is in specially close contact with his fellow-citizens imposes upon him special duties towards them—just as the even closer contact with parents, wife, children imposes upon him special duties towards his family. There is, then, a form of patriotism which is not only natural, but also right. Patriotism is wrong only when the country is deified and men's love for it becomes associated with pride and vanity on the one hand and contempt, suspicion and hatred on the other. The tree is known by its fruits, and a patriotism whose fruits are boasting and lying, swindling and stealing, threatening, bullying and, finally, wholesale murder, cannot conceivably be a good thing.

Circumstances cause us to feel a special love for and loyalty towards our country and impose, at the same time, special moral duties towards it. Among those duties is the duty to do all in one's power to preserve one's country from acting in ways which one knows to be wrong. It is a duty which, if we love our country, we shall undertake the more willingly; for nothing is more painful than to see a person one loves disgrace himself. The active pacifist is a better patriot than those imperialists and militarists who want their country to behave as a robber, a bully and a murderer. (See *Moral Equivalent of War; Nationalistic Religion.*)

88

The Peace Pledge Union

The Peace Pledge Union dates back to the day when Canon Sheppard invited any man who felt as he did to send him a post-card stating that he renounced war and would never again take part in another one. The invitation was given through the following letter which appeared in the Press on 16th October, 1934:—

The main reason for this letter, primarily addressed to men, is the fresh urgency of the present international situation, and the almost universally acknowledged lunacy of the manner in which nations are pursuing peace.

The situation is far graver than we allow ourselves to acknowledge, and the risks we are running by our present methods far graver than those which a more enlightened policy would involve.

Up to now the Peace Movement has received its main support from women, but it seems high time now that men should throw their weight into the scales against War.

I represent no Church and no peace organization of any description, but merely, I suggest, the mentality to which the average man has recently arrived without, as it seems, the knowledge of his accredited leaders in Church and State, or, for that matter, without their assistance.

It seems essential to discover whether or not it be true, as we are told, that the majority of thoughtful men in this country are now convinced that war of every kind or for any cause, is not only a denial of Christianity, but a crime against humanity, which is no longer to be permitted by civilized people.

Have we reached that state of belief?

I believe that we have, but I am certain that the time has come when we must know if that is a false or true statement.

The idea behind this letter is not to form any fresh organization, nor to call pacifists together to abuse those who conscientiously are not able to agree with them, but to attempt to discover how strong the will to peace has grown.

For myself, I believe that a vast number of male citizens who do

89

not belong to any peace society and even dislike some of the methods of those who do, are only waiting an opportunity to declare once and for all that they have done with wars of every kind.

Many persons are avowing their determination to use violence, not only between nations, but within the nations.

An ever-increasing dependence on excessive force is evident in the movements known as Communism and Fascism.

It is time that those men who have not hitherto acted in any public way, but who wish the repudiation of methods of violence, should come into the open.

Would those of my sex who, so far, have been silent, but are of this mind, send a post-card to me within the next fortnight, addressed to:—

East Lodge,
Ashley Park,
Walton-on-Thames,

to say if they are willing to be called together in the near future to vote in support of a resolution as uncompromising as the following:—

"We renounce War and never again, directly or indirectly, will we support or sanction another."

If the response to this letter be as large as conceivably it may be, a notice will be sent at the earliest possible moment with full particulars of the day and date on which the demonstration will be made.

The response was immediate and overwhelming. Cards began to come in at once, and there has been a constant stream of them ever since. By the end of the first twelve months the number of pledged members had reached a total of some 80,000, and by the beginning of 1937 it had grown to nearer 130,000.

So "Dick Sheppard's Army" was enlisted and the first demonstration which the original letter had promised was held at the Albert Hall in June, 1935, when over 7,000 men of all ages (many of them ex-Service men), most professions, and very different circumstances gathered

90

from all parts of the country to register their determination to have nothing more to do with war.

It was not long, however, before the question arose as to what effective use could be made of this answer to his personal appeal. He saw that it was no longer possible to regard it as a kind of private venture. By reason of its numerical and moral strength it has become a national movement. Canon Sheppard therefore invited some leading men and women to join him as sponsors, and it became the Peace Pledge Movement under the guidance of these sponsors, who to-day consist of Harold Bing, Vera Brittain, H. Runham Brown, General Crozier, James Hudson, Aldous Huxley, Storm Jameson, George Lansbury, Rose Macaulay, Stuart Morris, Philip Mumford, Lord Ponsonby, Charles Raven, Bertrand Russell, Siegfried Sassoon, H. R. L. Sheppard, Donald Soper, Arthur Wragg, Alex Wood and Wilfred Wellock.

So far the Movement had been confined to men, but the problems of Peace were obviously as much the concern of women as of men, and so the decision was taken to ask for the signatures of women.

Once more there was an immediate response, although the Press did not give the same publicity to this new phase as to the earlier letter. At first the women's pledge differed slightly from the men's, but henceforward there will be one common pledge—the simple renunciation of the war method in all circumstances. Both men and women are admitted on the same basis with the one reservation that it is intended to keep such a balance between the two sides of the Movement, that the number of women signatories will not be allowed to exceed the number of men signatories. So the Peace Pledge Union—

for such is its name to-day—covers the whole country and represents one of the biggest movements in our national life.

A start was made by taking temporary offices in Trafalgar Square. To-day, headquarters are housed in offices at 96, Regent Street, and Max Plowman has become General Secretary. Mr. John Barclay is acting as Group Organizer and it is hoped that area secretaries will be appointed in due course.

A word must be said about General Crozier, to whose care was entrusted the keeping of the records at the Recruiting Headquarters in his charge at Walton-on-Thames, where originally all the Pledge Cards were filed. With the acquisition of permanent headquarters in London, however, this department has been transferred to Regent Street.

In the meantime, the Union is busy with the organization of local groups. All over the country signatories have been asked to meet at some hall, easy of access, in order that they might get to know one another, and be put wise as to the aims of the Movement.

In many cases a Regional Committee links up the contiguous groups, and groups are dividing themselves into teams of ten to twenty members. It is within these groups and teams that the real work of the Peace Pledge Union must be done.

It is sometimes said that Pacifism is a mere negation; but if it begins with the refusal to take part in war, it does not and cannot end there. We have an obligation to work out the lines of constructive peace. To that end, Aldous Huxley wrote the first official pamphlet of the Movement, "What are you going to do about it?" explaining its aims and basis. Gerald Heard has written

92

a second which deals more with organization. Other pamphlets and leaflets have been written and are in preparation. There is ample material for the groups who are continuing courses of corporate study on the general aims of the Peace Movement or on any particular subject which may appeal to them; e.g. the Colonial problem, the New World Conference, etc. Groups also provide the opportunity for the exchange of views among their members, who can thus face up to individual difficulties and become equipped to answer attacks in the Press, etc. Members must be ready also to be missionaries and embark on propaganda through open-air and other meetings. Indeed, every individual member of a group can find some job that he or she can do; and all should be doing something. The Union now has its official paper in *Peace News*, which is published weekly. It is hoped that every member will become a regular subscriber and endeavour to secure an ever-increasing circulation.

Other ventures are worthy of note. The Union opened a shop in Ludgate Hill. Every day a large number of inquiries were dealt with, and for two different periods midday meetings were held in the basement. These were attended by a growing number of those whose work brought them to the City. The Union also opened an office in Brussels during the International Peace Congress in 1936. There its representatives were able to make contact with many Continental pacifists. The Union held a special meeting at the conclusion of the Congress, at which the aims, programme and methods were explained to a gathering consisting, in the main, of British and American delegates. A most useful conference was also held with leaders of Continental Pacifist

93

Organizations. Some twenty groups were represented, and there was a discussion on possible ways of co-ordination with special reference to a proposal to inaugurate an International Pacifist Movement.

At the beginning of 1937 the P.P.U. carried out an intensive campaign, in the course of which many of the large cities and towns in East England, Scotland and Wales were visited by a team of speakers who addressed large and enthusiastic meetings.

Later in the year an event of real significance to the peace movement occurred when the No More War Movement decided to abandon its separate identity and become merged in the P.P.U. To facilitate this, two of the No More War Movement representatives were added to the sponsors and an undertaking was given that as soon as an opportunity arose the whole movement should be given as democratic and representative a shape as possible. The actual constitution of the P.P.U. is being worked out and it is hoped that before long it will be finally approved and adopted.

It should be added that the P.P.U. is affiliated with the War Resisters' International, fuller particulars of which will be found elsewhere in this encylopædia.

The policy of the P.P.U. arises out of the basis of membership which is the renunciation of the war method. It is specially concerned with the present race in armaments and is taking every opportunity to protest at the British Armament proposals. Particularly it is asking that the public shall refuse to participate in the Anti Air Raid Precautions on the ground that they are inadequate, and calculated to develop a war mentality and prepare the way for the conscription of the Civil population. Further it is

94

concerned by the fact that the attempt to cure unemployment by rearmament means that many a man who has a conscientious objection to making arms is being offered war-work as the only method of ending a long period of enforced idleness.

It is recognized that it is not sufficient merely to say "No" to War. Pacifism must have a constructive policy and there is a moral obligation on the Union to work out such a positive programme. The P.P.U. would press for the immediate calling of a new World Conference at which the representatives of all *nations* (rather than governments) should be invited to sit on terms of absolute equality around the "family" table in order that their needs and grievances might be frankly discussed. If we are to avoid war we must be prepared to discuss all the causes of possible war in a spirit of understanding and sympathy. All cards must be laid on the table, and those who "have" must recognize their responsibility toward those who "have not." The P.P.U. would also press for a reconstructed League of all the Nations, with such a court of equity as would make possible an extension of the mandate system, and from the Covenant of which the territorial clauses of the Treaty of Versailles should be dissociated and the penal clauses eliminated. For the P.P.U. cannot support sanctions.

Its verdict against war is absolute and it repudiates the war method as much when used in Self-Defence or in support of the League and Collective Security as in actual aggression. It is prepared to press for a general refusal to supply the financial and material resources necessary for war-making to both parties to a dispute as a logical extension of the determination of its members not to take part in war. For, above all, the P.P.U. stands for the method of non-violent resistance. It is not just content to do nothing. It aims at so working out the technique of non-violent resistance that it will set free the new spirit and create the new attitude in the world. It is not a specifically Christian movement nor is there any credal or denominational test of membership. But it does see Pacifism in terms of a Faith. As it denies the right of material force and power to usurp the position of ultimate authority, so it seeks to appeal to spiritual and moral power. It is a fellowship of men and women who are prepared to study constructive peace-making, become enthusiastic missionaries in the cause, and accept such discipline as would be necessary if we are all going to repudiate in all relationships the destructive method of violence and prove the redeeming power of Love.

We are living in critical days. It is not enough to desire peace or to talk peace. We must make personal decisions and live peace.

Anyone, therefore, to whom this appears as a paramount issue, will find within the P.P.U. the ground on which he or she can meet with other pacifists, the encouragement of belonging to a great and growing movement, the fellowship within which is included the training of spirit, mind and body, essential if we are to rid the world of war. Peace cannot be made by Treaties, Pacts or Systems of Collective Security. It can only come when we create the conditions within which Peace is inevitable. The P.P.U. denies that war is inevitable—that it is anything but a sin, and it aims at creating those conditions which will make peace inevitable. It is therefore anxious to include within its membership and training everyone who is ready wholly to renounce war and to live instead for peace.

Peace Treaties

It is often said that war begets war. But it would be more correct to say that the Peace Treaties signed at the conclusion of a war almost invariably sow seeds of future conflicts. Of the Great War it has been quite fairly asserted that while we won the war we lost the peace. It is a good, although an extreme, instance showing how victors in their hour of triumph cannot act justly. They are thinking of the immediate past, not of the future; and punishment is the idea that is uppermost in their minds. The vanquished had been incessantly described while the war lasted as a criminal nation which was solely responsible for the war. Although this charge was, as time passed, qualified, mitigated, and finally no longer asserted, it was at the moment of triumph the dominant justification for punishment. Moreover, the people in the triumphant nations, wounded and suffering and still enflamed against the enemy, could be counted on to support the infliction of severe punishment. The atmosphere thus created was irresistible. Consequently purely punitive articles were inserted in the Treaties of Versailles and St. Germain, with the enthusiastic consent of the Allied and Associated Powers.

The payment of a fantastic indemnity was imposed on Germany, singled out as the chief culprit, unilateral disarmament was enforced on her, she was deprived of all her colonies, and her frontiers as well as those of her allies were adjusted according to strategic considerations to cramp and weaken their national life. In four years Germany had been beaten to her knees. In the sub-

97

sequent twenty years every effort had to be made to set her on her feet again. This process was too slow, although the victorious governments gradually realized that the creation of a danger spot of resentment and of a spirit of revenge, the natural result of their punishment, must dislocate the economic life of all nations and be a menace to world peace. So, as we now find, the Treaties are being scrapped bit by bit and the follies of Versailles and St. Germain are being retracted, lest the imposition of any of the penal clauses should lead to another war.

This example is fresh in our minds. Others could be quoted. Twenty-five years after the signature of the Treaty of Vienna (at the conclusion of the Napoleonic wars) only one clause delineating the frontiers of Switzerland remained in force.

Police Methods

War is often justified on the ground that when it is "in support of Law" (which means in practice when it is being waged by one's own country) it is no more than police action. (This was the view expressed by the Archbishop of York when arguing against pacifism.) Let us consider the differences between the police and the military:

(1) The police are generally unarmed. Their prime task is the prevention of crime and the forestalling of public disturbances.

(2) When a crime has been committed, or when trouble has broken out, the function of the police is to

arrest the person or persons who are guilty. They have no power of inflicting punishment and they are not permitted to use more force than is necessary to secure the arrest of the guilty party.

Armies are radically different from police forces.

(1) They are armed, and the more efficient their arms become, the more indiscriminate becomes the destruction which they inflict.

(2) The force which they are empowered to use is not limited. Their function is not to restrain the guilty; it is to destroy all things and people within their range. When the police wish to arrest a criminal, they do not burn up a town in which he is living and kill or torture all its inhabitants. But this precisely is what an army does, particularly an army using modern weapons.

(3) States arrogate to themselves the right, not only to judge other states, but also, by means of their armies, to punish them. The principle is wholly repugnant to law; moreover, the process of punishing a guilty nation entails the destruction of countless innocent individuals. An army with tanks and bombing squadrons is not and cannot be a police force. Nor can its essentially evil and destructive functions be moralized by calling it a League army, an instrument of collective security, etc. Police operate with the universal consent of the community which employs them. Armies operate at the order of one among the nations or the few nations which are allied together.

(See *Force; International Police Force; Sanctions.*)

Political Implications of Pacifism

The ultimate realities of the human world are individual men and women. Physically, all human beings belong to a single species and a spiritual unity underlies all their divergencies of native ability and acquired habit. These are the facts of experience upon which the pacifist bases his philosophy. His fundamental ethical principles spring from these facts and may be formulated thus: Human personality must be respected. Individuals, in the words of Kant, must always be regarded as ends in themselves, not as means. It is the duty of every man to do all in his power to realize in practice that fundamental human unity which is obscured by the organized greed and the organized hatred of our nationalisms, our religions and our economic systems.

The political implications of pacifism may be briefly summed up as follows:

(1) Democratic institutions. Pacifism is incompatible with any form of tyranny. Conversely war and preparation for war on the modern scale are incompatible with personal liberty and democratic institutions. In the world of to-day an enslaved country under a tyrant is an efficient war-machine; a democratically organized country is not. We are faced with the choice between preparation for war, accompanied by slavery, on the one hand, and pacifism, accompanied by personal liberty and democratic institutions, on the other.

(2) Decentralization. Democratic principles cannot be effectively put into practice except in a community where authority has been as far as possible decentralized. Another important point: it is hard in a decentralized

state for any one man to impose his will on the whole community. Social reform aims at taking away the opportunities for evil. In a decentralized state the ambitious man is not "led into temptation"; in other words, he is given few opportunities for indulging his ruling passions at the expense of others. It is of the utmost importance that the amount of power that can be wielded by any one individual should be strictly limited, and one of the great merits of decentralization is that it automatically does this. To place limitations on personal wealth and the private ownership of the means of production is desirable for the same reason.

(3) Local and professional self-government. Decentralization must be accompanied by self-government, not only in municipal matters but also in industry and the professions. Industrial organizations are, too often, miniature dictatorships. Respect for human personality demands that there should be decentralization into self-governing groups in all the trades and professions. In many cases, as Dubreuil has shown in his interesting book, *A Chacun sa Chance*, decentralization into self-governing groups leads, not only to more satisfactory human relations, but also to greater efficiency.

(4) Improvement of social services and extension of educational facilities. It is unnecessary to elaborate this point.

(5) Disarmament, unilateral if necessary. Liquidation of empire, either by liberations of subject peoples or by transference of control, under a genuine mandate system to international authority.

(6) Removal of barriers to international trade. (See *Economic Implications of Pacifism*.)

Prestige and National Honour

Prestige is the diplomatic name for vanity. In individuals, vanity is regarded as stupid and contemptible. In nations it is regarded as something admirable. Owing to our double system of morality, we condemn the man whose actions are motivated by vanity; but the nation which goes to war for the sake of its prestige (in other words, for the sake of national vanity) is regarded as reasonable and even noble.

Whenever questions of national honour and prestige are being discussed, it is good to remember the following points:

(1) The nation is not a person and is therefore incapable of having the feelings which politicians and journalists like to attribute to it. The nation consists of a collection of individual men and women. To say that the nation has feelings and a will apart from the feelings and wills of individuals composing it, is false.

(2) The ruling classes find that they can consolidate their power by representing the nation as a kind of superhuman person with feelings and a will of its own. As representatives of this superhuman person, they partake of its divinity and they are able, by means of propaganda, to persuade the masses that what they, the rulers, want to do is what the divine, national person wants to do.

(3) The ruling classes are much more preoccupied with questions of national prestige than the masses. The reasons for this are of various kinds. (a) Being rulers, they tend to associate themselves with the nation they control. Its successes are their successes; its failures are their failures. National prestige is largely the personal

102

prestige of the nation's diplomats, ministers, civil servants and the like. (*b*) National prestige is in many cases associated with colonial possessions. Colonial possessions offer a particularly attractive field for the speculative investor. Colonies may not be profitable to the community which owns them; often, indeed, they are a burden on the taxpayers of the colonizing country. In many cases, however, they are extremely profitable to a small class of financiers, who find that they can get very high yields for their money in colonial enterprises. Another class which profits by the existence of colonies is the class from which administrators are drawn. These people get a secure income out of their country's colonial possessions and, more important, an opportunity to exercise power in a way which would be impossible at home. Not unnaturally, the members of these two classes are keen imperialists, and feel that any threat to a colonial possession is a threat to the nation's honour and prestige. Newspapers are owned and edited by members of these two classes. Newspaper opinion is therefore intensely preoccupied with questions of national honour and prestige. But newspaper opinion is not the opinion of the masses. To ordinary working men and women it would be a matter of almost complete indifference if the Japanese, for example, were to seize Hong-Kong. They would not feel that national honour was compromised and they would not feel that it was worth while, for the sake of prestige, to send their sons to go and murder and be murdered in a far-eastern battle. If they knew how Hong-Kong had been acquired, they would feel even less concern about the keeping up of British prestige. Hong-Kong was ceded to us at the

103

end of the war which we fought in order to compel the Chinese Government to take the opium which we were growing in India. The Chinese Government regarded opium as a curse and tried to stop the trade. The British Government compelled the Chinese to take opium by force of arms. When the war was over, Hong-Kong was seized as an indemnity. National honour, it must be admitted, is a very curious commodity.

Propaganda

On the outbreak of war it is as necessary to inflame public opinion into a state of indignation and hatred of her enemy as it is to supply the fighting forces with munitions. The case against the enemy must be stated with complete bias and a suitable amount of exaggeration. Any arguments in support of the enemy's case must be suppressed. As early as possible atrocities perpetrated by the enemy must be circulated and the enemy's cruel treatment of prisoners described in order to prevent desertions. In the official circular issued during the Great War, when an endeavour was made to collect the necessary material, it was written: "Essential not literal truth and correctness are necessary. Inherent probability being respected, the thing imagined may be as serviceable as the thing seen." Lies, therefore, are circulated by each government to stir up resentment in their people. In a country which has not conscription they have to be more lurid and more frequent than in conscripted nations. Faked photographs are useful and studios for the photography of hideous mutilations can be set up. A good catch-phrase is of special value. In the Great War the Kaiser's supposed reference to the British expeditionary force as "the contemptible little army" helped recruiting more than any other effort that was made. It was only discovered after the war was over that he never said anything of the kind and was not even at the place where he was supposed to have made this statement. No invention about the enemy published independently by the press is ever checked. But any attempt to plead for peace or to say a good word for the enemy may be ruthlessly punished.

It will thus be seen that there was unlimited use, not only of physical violence, but also of fraud. Lies are as necessary in war as shells or planes. Meanwhile militarists assure us that war is the school of virtue. (Consult *Falsehood in Wartime*, by Lord Ponsonby.)

Where the intervals of peace are used for the preparation of fresh wars, propaganda also plays an important part. It is a significant fact that it is precisely in those countries where military preparations are carried on most intensively that truth is most carefully distorted and suppressed. In the liberal countries there is no official peace-time censorship, such as exists in the totalitarian states. But this does not mean, unhappily, that there is no suppression or distortion of truth in the press of these countries. Newspapers are now run almost exclusively for profit. The result is that nothing must be printed that may dry up the sources of profit. Anything which might frighten away advertisers is kept out of the papers. Nor must we forget the power of the socially irresponsible rich men who own newspapers. These men dictate policy to their editors according to the whim of the moment or their own pecuniary interests. Private, plutocratic censorship takes the place in liberal countries of the official state censorship of totalitarian countries. Luckily, the whims and the financial interests of the plutocrats are not identical. What one suppresses, another allows to appear. More truth gets through in the liberal than in the totalitarian countries. Still, the system in both is thoroughly vicious. (Consult Hamilton Fyfe's *Press Parade*.)

Racialism

Racialism is the belief that certain human groups, commonly and often erroneously called races, have in respect of all their members innate mental or moral differences from other groups.

Where these groups are races in the scientific sense, where, that is to say, there are well-defined physical differences between one group and another, it is possible that these physical differences have mental or moral counterparts. It may be, for example, that the physiological causes which produce red hair and an aquiline nose are linked with qualities of the inner man different from those linked with black hair and a snub nose. But while this may be the case, the attempts which have hitherto been made to prove it cover far too narrow a field of investigation for their results to be accepted with any confidence.

Racialism, however, as it is popularly understood, has little to do with race as scientifically defined. The Jews are regarded as a race, yet they are a community

106

of the most diverse physical types, united only by a common religion and to some extent a similar environment. The "Latin races" consist of people of various types, united only by the fact that their ancestors were thoroughly conquered by the Romans. The "British race" is descended from a score of immigrant waves, offshoots of larger groups which remained outside.

It is impossible to suppose that such groups possess innate qualities except by completely ignoring the effect of environment upon character.

Revolution

Left Wing pacifists denounce the violence of capitalists, but consider that any violence used by themselves or their friends in defence of a socialist community against foreign aggressors, or, within a capitalist community, against the ruling classes is fully justified. Let us consider these two contingencies.

(1) In modern air warfare there is no defence except counter-attack, directed against the centres of population. If a socialist state is attacked, its airmen must go and drop fire and poison on the enemy's cities. It is extremely unlikely that they will ever kill a member of the enemy's capitalist government, for the good reason that governments always take extremely good care to remove themselves to places of safety. The people who will bear the brunt of the socialist airmen's attack will be workers and their wives and children. Thus, the proletarian state will be "defended" by the wholesale slaughter of proletarians.

Another point: a socialist state which is to wage war successfully against its enemies must be at least as well organized, for military purposes, as they are. But high military efficiency cannot be achieved except by resorting to policies which are essentially fascist and imperialistic in character. Military efficiency demands extreme concentration of power, a high degree of centralization, the training of the masses in passive obedience to their superiors, the imposition of some form of conscription or slavery to the state, and the creation of a local idolatry with the nation or a semi-deified tyrant as the object of worship. The defence of Socialism against Fascism by military means entails the transformation of the socialist community into a fascist community. Even before war has broken out, the process of military preparation will have transformed the liberty, the justice, the democracy for whose sake violence is to be used, into slavery, hierarchical privilege and tyranny. During the war and after it, the state of things will of course be much worse than before. There is only one method of defence which will not transform socialism into its opposite, and that is the method of non-violent resistance. A socialist community of men and women educated to be free and self-reliant, and trained in the methods of non-violence as intensively as they are now being trained in the methods of violence could allow a foreign army to invade its territory and still put up a defence of socialism that would have a good chance of being successful. Military defence, on the contrary, has no chance whatsoever of being successful. Even if the socialists win the war they will long since have ceased to be socialists. Nor will they be able, after victory, to return to their principles. Surrounded by defeated enemies, all thirsting for revenge, they will have to go on preparing for future wars.

(2) Tanks, planes, gases and thermite have made nonsense of the old revolutionary tactics. The days of the barricade are over. No violent revolutionary movement can hope to be successful unless it disposes of modern armaments and the services of technicians. Where both sides have modern weapons, revolution becomes a civil war (as in Spain), and there is massacre and destruction on an enormous scale.

Social revolution is a movement for humanity and against all that is base and inhuman. A social revolution that is prepared to slaughter and destroy is a contradiction in terms; a bloody revolution is not a change for the better, it is a repetition of all that is worst and least human in the existing order. Moreover, if the revolution is to slaughter efficiently, it must be organized on a military basis, that is, it must become a fascist dictatorship. Karl Marx called violence "The midwife of a new order of society." The facts do not bear this out. Violence begets violence and is therefore the perpetuator of the old order. Barthélemy de Ligt has summed up the whole matter in a single phrase: the more violence, the less revolution.

Advantages of non-violent resistance. (1) In the modern world the masses are not in a position to use violence as effectively as the ruling classes. It is by the use of non-violent tactics, including the refusal to work, to pay taxes, to buy certain classes of goods that the masses can resist oppression most effectively. (2) Violence on the modern scale destroys vast numbers of lives and

109

vast amounts of accumulated wealth (buildings, railways, machinery, etc.). The casualties among non-violent resisters may be high; but it is unlikely, as history shows, that they will be as high as in a violent struggle. Where non-violent resistance is used, there is no destruction of accumulated wealth. (3) The use of violence leads to a definite lowering of moral standards, a definite dehumanization of individuals participating in the slaughter and destruction. The use of non-violence leads, as was clearly demonstrated in South Africa, in Corea, in India, to a raising of the human level among all concerned.

Objections to the use of non-violent tactics:

(1) "They are not effective." Answer: If sufficient numbers, sufficiently well trained, employ non-violent methods, they are effective. The non-violent opposition of the Hungarians to Austrian oppression (1861–7), the non-violent resistance put up by the Indians in Natal against the oppression of the South African government (1907–13), the non-violent refusal of the Finns to submit to conscription (1902), the non-violent action of English workmen protesting against the Government's military campaign against Bolshevik Russia—these were all fully successful. The Hungarians were given all they demanded; the Finns were not conscribed; the iniquitous legislation against the Hindus was repealed; and the British Government was forced to abandon its military activities against Russia.

(2) "It would take a very long time to carry through a revolution by non-violent means." Answer: It will probably take even longer to carry it through by violence. Indeed, there is good reason to believe that a genuine revolution can never be carried out violently. The

110

French revolution used violence and resulted in a temporary military dictatorship and the permanent imposition upon all Frenchmen of military slavery, or conscription. The Russian revolution used violence; and to-day, Russia is a military dictatorship. It looks as though genuine revolution, that is, the change from the inhuman to the human, could not be effected by means of violence.

(3) "The cases already cited prove how difficult it is to induce people to use non-violent methods." Answer: Every people is conditioned by its history. Long oppressed by the Tsars, living in a badly organized society which, in 1917, had been reduced to anarchy, the Russians were probably foredoomed by their history to make use of violence in their revolution. This is not true of the peoples of the Western democracies. Thanks to the Quakers and other sects of Protestant Christians, the English have long been familiar with pacifist ideas. They have not, in recent times, had to suffer very violent oppression, while habits of humanitarianism are well established in English society. The organization of non-violent action in favour of a genuine social revolution would not be very difficult in England. The same is true of such countries as Holland, Denmark, Norway, Sweden, and to a lesser extent of Belgium and France. (See *Civil War; Force; Non-Violence.*)

Sanctions

The moral problem of Sanctions is the moral problem of war. Economic sanctions cannot remain merely economic; applied with vigour, they can only lead to war. Sanctionists try to conceal this fact by calling their brand of war by high-sounding names. We must not be deceived by words. "Collective security" means, in the circumstance of to-day, a system of opposed alliances. And "international police force" is merely a composite army furnished by a group of allied powers. As for "military sanctions"—they are plain war; and war is always war, whatever you may choose to call it.

Once war has broken out, nations will take sides or remain neutral according to their national interests, not as any international covenant dictates. Speaking at Leamington (November 20, 1936) Mr. Eden stated that "our armaments may be used in bringing help to a victim of aggression in any case where, in our judgment, it would be proper under the provisions of the Covenant to do so. I use the word 'may' deliberately since in such an instance there is no automatic obligation to take military action. It is, moreover, right that this should be so, for nations cannot be expected to incur automatic military obligations save for areas where their vital interests are concerned." This means that, in practice, a League war against an aggressor would be simply a war between two groups of allied powers, with other neutral powers looking on. Sanctionists believe that the mere display of a great military force would be enough to deter would-be aggressors. The greater your force, the slighter the probability that you will have to use it; therefore, they argue, rearm for the sake of peace. The facts of history do not bear out this contention. Threats do not frighten the determined nor do the desperate shrink before a display of overwhelming force.

Moreover, in the contemporary world, there is no reason to suppose that the force mustered against an aggressor will be overwhelming. The "League" and the "aggressor" will be two well-matched sets of allied powers.

"Military sanctions" are to be applied in order to bring about a just settlement of disputes. But the prospects of achieving a just settlement at the end of a League war are no better than at the end of an ordinary war. Passions run so high during war, that it is morally certain that the final settlement will be unjust and that another war will break out as soon as the conquered feel strong enough to take their revenge.

Not only would sanctions fail to produce the results they are meant to produce; they cannot even be applied. The neighbours of aggressor states will always be deterred from applying even economic sanctions by the thought that they will be the first to suffer reprisals. Countries will fight only when their vital interests are involved. Upholding the League Covenant is not regarded by any nation as a vital interest. Those who refuse to enforce sanctions against an aggressor have themselves infringed the Covenant. Who is going to enforce sanctions against *them*?

Morality and practical common sense are at one in demanding that Article XVI should be omitted from the Covenant and that the League should concentrate on active co-operative work for removing the causes of war. The attempt to cure war, once it has broken out, by means of Sanctions (that is, more war) is foredoomed to failure.

(See *International Police Force; League of Nations, The.*)

Secret Treaties

When war is declared the nation is likely to have the support of declared allies, but it will also wish to enlist the support of other nations. It therefore becomes necessary to decide on division of the spoils in the event of victory. The history of the Great War provides numerous examples of Secret Treaties concluded in these circumstances. Between 1915 and 1917 secret engagements were entered into between this country and France, Italy, Japan, Roumania, Russia, Serbia and Montenegro, covering a very large field of possible conquests which might be expected.

To mention only two of the more important stipulations: By the secret Treaty of London, signed in April 1915, Italy was to receive the Trentino and the Tyrol as far as the Brenner, Trieste and Istria, all the Dalmatian coast except Fiume, full ownership of Vallona and a protectorate over the rest of Albania, a "just share" of Turkey and "equitable compensation" in Africa. A few weeks earlier Russia had been promised Constantinople, several Mediterranean islands and bits of Thrace and Asia Minor.

The text of these Treaties was discovered in the archives of the Russian Foreign Office and published by the Russian Government after the revolution. They illustrate very clearly the fact that, once war has broken out, all considerations of justice disappear. Nothing matters any more except victory and, to secure victory, governments are prepared to make the most cynically immoral arrangements with anyone whose aid can be bought.

(See *Secret Treaties*, by F. Seymour Cocks (Union of Democratic Control). Temperley, *History of the Peace Conference*, Vols. 5 and 6.)

Shelley

In 1819 a meeting in favour of parliamentary reform, held in the Peterloo Fields at Manchester, was broken up by a cavalry charge. Six persons were killed and many injured. When the news reached Shelley, who was living in Italy at the time, "it roused in him," says Mrs. Shelley, "violent emotions of indignation and compassion." The great truth that the many, if accordant and resolute, could control the few, as was shown a few days later, made him long to teach his injured countrymen how to resist. Inspired by these feelings, he wrote *The Mask of Anarchy*. The method of resistance inculcated by Shelley in *The Mask of Anarchy* is the method of non-violence.

> Stand ye calm and resolute,
> Like a forest, close and mute,
> With folded arms and looks that are
> Weapons of unvanquished war. . . .
>
> And if then the tyrants dare,
> Let them ride among you there,
> Slash, and stab, and maim and hew—
> What they like, that let them do.
>
> With folded arms and steady eyes,
> And little fear, and less surprise,
> Look upon them as they slay
> Till their rage has passed away.

Then they will return with shame
To the place from which they came
And the blood thus shed will speak
In hot blushes on their cheek.

Every woman in the land
Will point at them as they stand—
They will hardly dare to greet
Their acquaintance in the street.

And that slaughter to the Nation
Shall steam up like inspiration,
Eloquent, oracular,
A volcano heard afar.

Rise like Lions after slumber
In unvanquishable number—
Shake your chains to earth like dew
Which in sleep had fallen on you—
Ye are many—they are few.

War Resisters' International

The Peace Pledge Union is affiliated to the War
Resisters' International and has now become the British
Section. But there are forty-nine other sections in
twenty-four different countries—some of them large
national movements, others quite small. Some are legal
and work openly with much publicity, others are illegal
and have to work underground. The International
extends into sixty-eight countries in all of which it has
its members and correspondents.

THE DECLARATION

The Declaration adopted at the first meeting of the International in 1921 and confirmed at each successive Conference since, is: "War is a crime against humanity. We therefore are determined not to support any kind of war and to strive for the removal of all causes of war." To this Declaration each member subscribes.

A very remarkable Statement of Principles was drawn up at the first meeting fifteen years ago and finally adopted at the First International Conference in 1925. This statement is so comprehensive that no change has been desired and no addition made to it. Were this statement re-written to-day—1937—reference might be made to war to defend democracy or war for an ideal, but our Statement of Principles leaves us in no doubt. The War Resisters' International, while often impelled to sympathy with one side in a conflict more than with the other, recognizes that the resort to armed violence, or any form of warfare, is damaging most of all to the "good cause."

STATEMENT OF PRINCIPLES

WAR IS A CRIME AGAINST HUMANITY.

It is a crime against life, and uses human personalities for political and economic ends.

WE, THEREFORE,

actuated by an intense love of mankind,

ARE DETERMINED NOT TO SUPPORT

either directly by service of any kind in the army, navy, or air forces, or indirectly by making or consciously handling munitions or other war material, subscribing to war loans or using our labour for the purpose of setting others free for war service.

aggressive or defensive, remembering that modern wars are invariably alleged by Governments to be defensive.

Wars would seem to fall under three heads:

(*a*) *Wars to defend the State* to which we nominally belong and wherein our home is situated. To refuse to take up arms for this end is difficult:

    1. Because the State will use all its coercive powers to make us do so.

    2. Because our inborn love for home has been deliberately identified with love of the State in which it is situated.

(*b*) *Wars to preserve the existing order of society* with its security for the privileged few. That we would never take up arms for this purpose goes without saying.

(*c*) *Wars on behalf of the oppressed proletariat*, whether for its liberation or defence. To refuse to take up arms for this purpose is most difficult:

    1. Because of the proletarian régime, and, even more, the enraged masses, in time of revolution would regard as a traitor anyone who refused to support the New Order by force.

    2. Because our instinctive love for the suffering and the oppressed would tempt us to use violence on their behalf.

However, we are convinced that violence cannot really *preserve order*, *defend* our home, or *liberate* the proletariat. In fact, experience has shown that in all wars, order, security, and liberty disappear, and that, so far from benefiting by them, the proletariat always suffer most.

We hold, however, that consistent pacifists have no right to take up a merely negative position, but *must recognize*

AND STRIVE FOR THE REMOVAL OF ALL THE CAUSES OF
WAR.

We recognize as causes of war not only the instinct of egoism and greed, which is found in every human heart, but also all agencies which create hatred and antagonism between groups of people. Among such, we would regard the following as the more important to-day:

1. Differences between *races*, leading by artificial aggravation to envy and hatred.

2. Differences between *religions*, leading to mutual intolerance and contempt.

3. Differences between the *classes*, the possessing and the non-possessing, leading to civil war, which will continue so long as the present system of production exists, and private profit rather than social need is the outstanding motive of society.

4. Differences between *nations*, due largely to the present system of production, leading to world wars and such economic chaos as we see to-day, which eventualities, we are convinced, could be prevented by the adoption of a system of world economy which had for its end the well-being of the entire human race.

5. Finally, we see an important cause of war in the prevalent misconception of the State. The State exists for man, not man for the State. The recognition of the sanctity of human personality must become the basic principle of human society. Furthermore, the State is not a sovereign self-contained entity, as every nation is a part of the great family of mankind. We feel, therefore, that consistent pacifists have no right to take up a merely negative position, but must devote themselves to abolishing classes, barriers between the peoples, and to creating a world-wide brotherhood founded on mutual service.

War Resistance is not an end in itself, it is a way of life to achieve an end. The goal, in the expression of the Socialist is, Liberty, Equality, Fraternity; in that of the Christian it is, Truth, Beauty, Love, a world where all can and will desire to co-operate for the common good.

THE COST TO THE INTERNATIONAL

There are 493 war resisters in the prisons of Europe alone, young men who have resolutely resisted the conscription laws of their country and who face loss of liberty, ostracism, poverty and often death. Many thousands have passed through prison, many have died in prison or after release. You are not asked to pity them, you will need all your pity for the soldier boys blindly led to the shambles. The man in prison you can respect, look up to him as your leader in the struggle.

THE WORK OF THE INTERNATIONAL

The International is guided by a Council which is elected for three years at the Triennial Conference which meets in a different country each time. The paid staff number three, the voluntary staff thirty-six. The budget is a little over £1,450 per annum and is raised by voluntary contributions.

The War Resisters' International has become a clearing house of ideas as well as a practical centre for the transfer of letters between countries where there is not even a postal convention providing for direct mail or where censors are too difficult to avoid. The International acts as a banker, holding contra accounts to overcome the restrictions on transfer of currency. It serves the Movement in innumerable ways.

Sometimes it does big jobs, sending its representatives to International Labour Movements, Conferences and even to Governments.

The International has to speak in many tongues. Fourteen languages are normally used and for this the

120

services of twenty-eight voluntary translators have been enlisted who work regularly for the movement.

The War Resisters' International publishes its quarterly bulletin, *The War Resister*, in French, German, English and Esperanto, together with much other literature. Every publication goes into Russia in the Russian language. Several publications in Spanish are at the disposal of Spanish comrades both in Spain and South America. Literature in Italian finds its way into Italy, while reprints appear in a dozen other languages.

THE SECTIONS OF THE INTERNATIONAL

No adequate idea of the Sections and their work can be given here. Many are illegal, their work has to be carried on with great care and our members take very considerable personal risks. The International often has to take over all records and not only keep direct contact with the leaders of sections, but with thousands of individual members. This work cannot be reported here.

In more democratic countries the movement has grown rapidly in recent years. In Denmark, for instance, where the membership has been doubled each year for several years—4,000 members in a little population of only one million is considerable. The U.S.A. has 10,000 members in one Section and many thousands in another. In Canada, 2,000 have signed the Peace Pledge Union's Declaration and the International has had to take over direct contact pending the formation of the Canadian Peace Pledge Union.

Space is quite inadequate to convey the immensity of this world-wide family, living a way of life, forerunners of a Revolution that will one day make of the world a garden where all shall co-operate for the good of all.

Women in Modern War, Position of

Between 1914 and 1918 the part played by women in carrying on the war was considerable. In France, for example, towards the end of the war, 1,500,000 women were employed in the war industries alone. In England the number of women employed in industry at large was about three millions. Of these, a considerable proportion worked in munition factories. Most of the rest took the place of men who were thus released for military service.

In the last war, women gave their services voluntarily. In the next, they will almost certainly be subject to conscription. In the words of a French military writer, Colonel Émile Mayer, "It is the function of the military authority to exploit its human materials [sic] as best it can, in the interests of national defence, without regard to the age of the individuals." Again, in time of national crisis, every citizen "is at the disposal of the State, whatever his or her sex." In any future war there will be, not merely military conscription, but also industrial, intellectual and moral conscription: and the whole population, women, children and the aged, as well as men, will be subjected to this State-imposed slavery. War is no longer an affair conducted by a small body of professionals; it has become totalitarian. Women are as intimately concerned in it as men.

Index

123

124

Printed in Great Britain by Butler & Tanner Ltd., Frome and London

WHAT ARE YOU GOING TO DO ABOUT IT?

Aldous Huxley

In this short but brilliant pamphlet Mr. Huxley raises, and answers, every argument which can be put forward in exoneration of war : each is dealt with so swiftly, lucidly and with such effect that a copy could profitably be in the hands of every public speaker interested in the great cause of international friendship.

To the individual in search of good *reasons* for his belief in peace it is a vade-mecum, and although short, it is not the least of Mr. Huxley's contributions to the statement of contemporary opinion.

Price Threepence

CHATTO & WINDUS: LONDON